EARTH, FAITH AND MISSION
The Theology and Practice of Earthcare

CLIVE AYRE

MOSAIC PRESS

Published in Australia by
Mosaic Press
508 High St
Preston Vic. 3072
Australia

Mosaic Press is an imprint of Mosaic Resources Pty Ltd

ISBN 9781743241189

First published 2013

Cataloguing-in-Publication entry is available for the National Library of Australia http:/catalogue.nla.gov.au/.

Book design by John Healy
Printed and bound in Great Britain by
Marston Book Services Limited, Oxfordshire

ACKNOWLEDGMENTS

Much of the material in this book had its origin in my retirement project, namely a PhD at the University of Queensland. I gladly acknowledge the support and encouragement I received in that project from Associate Professor Neil Pembroke in particular. From the inception of the research, and through many conversations, his friendship, questions, and probing have been most valuable. I am also grateful to Assoc. Prof. Richard Hutch, to members of my PhD group, to people both in the United Kingdom and in Australia whom I consulted during the course of the research, and to those many friends, old and new, with whom, in one way or another, I have shared the journey. My thanks go to a number of friends and colleagues who have willingly read the manuscript and given me some valuable feedback. My son Ian, whose own academic journey has led him in a related area of research, has always been an interested and informed conversation partner in the project; but I am grateful to my whole family for their interest, love, and support. Most of all, I want to acknowledge my wife Gail, who urged me strongly to undertake the project in the first place, and whose constant loving support means more than I could say.

Clive W Ayre

For my Grandchildren
Natalie, Jeremy, Alexander, David,
Joshua, Rebecca, Zachary,
Lily, William and Hamish

With the prayer that the responses we make now will enable them and
their generation to enjoy a sustainable environment in the future.

Contents

CHAPTER ONE

Introduction

The Beginning of a Journey

I have sometimes thought about what it is that has motivated me to set out on this road of environmental care, and I think that at a conscious level the journey began one afternoon in 1988 when our son indicated to us that his high school had decided to nominate him for the Lions Youth of the Year competition. Among other things, that involved the preparation and delivery of a speech on a subject of his choosing. So having been inspired by his geography teacher, our son chose to speak about threats to the environment; it was a speech we were to hear a number of times as he proceeded through stages of the competition. For him it was to lead not only to a passion for the environment, but also to a postgraduate qualification in environmental education. Thus it was that through this process my own awareness of and concern about environmental issues received an important impetus.

In the early 1990's I had the opportunity to build on that beginning through the completion of an MA degree on the theme, *"Christ and Creation: Towards a Theology of Creation and Redemption in the Context of Ecological Crisis"*. The fundamental aim of the thesis was to consider what it means to believe in God as Creator in the face of the emerging eco-crisis. That work established some of the theological underpinnings of the issue, including historical factors, and demonstrated that the notions of creation and redemption must be held together in theology, spirituality, and service, with very real implications for the environment. I was able to build on that work in my subsequent PhD research on *"An Approach to Ecological Mission in and through the Christian Community in Australia: Beyond Apathy to Committed Action."*

Since that time there have been a number of significant developments, two of which may be mentioned here. First, while there are still some who deny or query climate change, it has become increasingly apparent that the global situation is deteriorating, and that the natural environment on which all life depends is in trouble. That in itself is of course a multi-faceted problem, and will be addressed in chapter 2. Nevertheless there is mounting evidence to support a growing consensus not only about the basic facts of the crisis, but also about human responsibility in creating or at least exacerbating the problem. Thus, for example, in the area of global warming, Dupont and Pearman in their 2006 Lowy Institute report are prepared to state that "there is no longer much doubt that the world is facing a prolonged period of planetary warming, largely fuelled by modern lifestyles, which is unprecedented in human history…", although their claim that "with a few notable exceptions, even sceptics now seem prepared to accept the validity of the basic science underpinning climate change forecasts"[1] may seem a little less certain. Governments in Australia have set up instrumentalities to deal with climate change issues, although they are also prone to scepticism including the unfortunate decision in 2013 to dismantle the Climate Commission in Australia. Nevertheless, scarcely a day goes by without a news story on the subject. More than that, the substantial increase in the volume of eco-theological literature over recent decades represents a significant development.

Second, in spite of excessive nationalism in some parts of the world, I think we are more aware of a global focus. Even though our initial concern may be the immediate impact of environmental negatives on our own region, the global nature of the crisis is important in the sense that what happens in one particular nation impacts not only on that nation, but also on the earth as a whole. Thus, one of the factors at work in spreading desert in Africa may be the destruction of the Amazon rainforest in South America; and the massive emissions of carbon dioxide from coal-fired plants in places like Australia, the United States or China impacts not only on those particular nations, but have global implications as well.

When we pause to think about it, there ought to be plenty to motivate us to begin this journey, beginning with a concern for those people who are most vulnerable as well as those wild creatures at risk of extinction. And it

---

1 Alan Dupont and Graeme Pearman. *Heating up the Planet: Climate Change and Security.* (Double Bay, NSW: Lowy Institute for International Policy, 2006), vii.

is a journey we must undertake, because quite apart from the science and the evidence all about us, we have a duty of care that has its origin in God.

For me personally, perhaps the real journey began long before 1988. As a Minister first of the Methodist Church and subsequently of the Uniting Church, I have been concerned about and involved in the mission of the Church in a whole range of theoretical, practical, and ecumenical ways for well over 40 years. My concern has been for the theological integrity of that mission at all levels. I have also been concerned about the historical tendency for the scope of Christian mission to be understood in relatively narrow terms, rather than, for example, in the light of Jesus' more holistic image of the Kingdom of God.

I am able to draw some consolation at least from the fact that ecological and environmental issues have started to show on the radar of the Christian community generally, although there is still a long way to go. That certainly appears to be the case in Australia, where such awareness seems to reflect a minority position. Consequently it seemed a natural step to bring together these dual concerns about the global environment and the mission of the Church.

Thus, at the risk of stating the obvious, it should be clear that I am approaching this book from the perspective of a committed Christian faith, and a desire to see individual Christians and the Church as a whole playing an effective and positive role in response to global issues and the imperatives of a sound theology of mission. However, that should not be interpreted as implying a dogmatic approach to theology; as I will make clear, effective eco-mission may be built upon a range of differing philosophical and theological positions. If the main goal is kept in view, partnerships may be built across some of the traditional divisions, both in the community at large and certainly within the Christian community.

But at a very personal level, probably the most immediate motivating focus would have to be that as a father and a grandfather I have become increasingly concerned about the quality of life my grandchildren will have; I may be spared the worst impact of a deteriorating environment, but they won't. So if I can do something about it for their sake and the generations to come, I will.

What the Book is About

This book is about a crisis. The term "crisis" can be overused, but this *is* a crisis, and the point of beginning is twofold. At one level there is clearly an environmental situation which, as I have already suggested, is increasingly recognised as a crisis that is real, significant, and global in character. We will ignore that at our great cost.

But at another level we might begin with the divine imperative that we should care for creation. We cannot continue to abuse and trash that which God has created and called good. More precisely therefore, this book is not only about a crisis facing life on Earth, but also about our response; it is about ways of understanding and living in which Christians can make a real difference. It is therefore a book about possibilities and hope.

I will introduce the nature and scope of the crisis in chapter 2, although it will be an illustrative rather than an in-depth look at aspects of the global ecology, including the effects and implications of climate change. But I suggest that social justice issues are also involved as an integral part of the crisis. The Christian Church is inevitably part of this crisis, and must be part of any solution. I will then discuss the significance of the assumptions we make, for example, when we read the Scriptures, and describe briefly a practical approach to doing theology. Our duty of care requires us to consider some important aspects of the partnership between faith and science.

Chapter 3 introduces a range of responses to environmental issues, beginning with a discussion on three largely unhelpful approaches to the natural environment – nature disenchanted, an econocentric approach, and a human-centred or an anthropocentric approach to the natural environment. A life-centred or biocentric approach is expressed in several different ways, including through indigenous spirituality. We then explore a theocentric or God-centred approach, or more precisely one that is both God and life centred; elements of both are combined in describing the most helpful way forward. Our perception of humankind as part of the overall "web of life" as well as our understanding of God is part of this.

We begin chapter 4 with what Paul Santmire described as "the ambiguous theological heritage of Christian theology", and I will go on to identify a number of critical issues which have often led to misunderstanding. I will then outline the importance of a theological approach as it relates key theological concepts to the care of creation. In this way we begin to see that eco-mission is theologically rather than crisis driven and is an essential element of the Church's life and mission.

In chapter 5 we move towards an eco-mission theology. Once our way of viewing life and the cosmos has been clarified, we can consider how we may respond to the issues confronting us. I will therefore look briefly at six options, and propose that a modified version of the stewardship model is the most helpful. "Mission" has proved difficult to define, but I will propose a way forward in which Habel's "Three Missions of the Church"[2] becomes a useful tool. The First Mission, "saving souls", is limited to the ultimate wellbeing of the individual. The Second Mission extends the field of concern to the whole person in context, so that issues of social justice are involved. The Third Mission encompasses the whole Earth, and this is developed in terms of an eco-mission theology that may be the basis of legitimate practical action.

Chapter 6 sets the scene in a different way; it illustrates the largely common mind reflected through international and ecumenical leadership as well as through national responses in Australia. A strong degree of confessional consensus in Earth-care extends also to the interfaith area. Denominational hierarchies also can play a positive role in promoting environmental care. The chapter outlines aspects of state-level and regional eco-mission, the role of peak organisations, the valuable role of an eco awards scheme, and concludes with the possible development of networks.

In chapter 7 we explore the way in which eco-mission may develop locally, beginning with the attitudes conducive to that. Several accounts of how it began in Australian congregations illustrate the point. This is followed by the significance of a small eco group to encourage the congregation as a whole, the importance of having an eco-mission statement, and several stories illustrating how one person can make a real difference. We will then catch a glimpse of what eco-mission looks like at a local or congregational level; this will include a thematic approach and include some stories of practical eco-mission. I conclude the chapter with some discussion on significant eco-mission inhibitors and the dynamics involved when earth

---

2 Norman C Habel. *The Third Mission of the Church*. In "Trinity Occasional Papers" (Trinity Theological College, Brisbane, 1998 XVII, I), 31-43.

mission initiatives fail. Strategies for maintaining the momentum of effective earth mission need to be understood and developed.

The final chapter raises the important issue of hope, and attempts to sum up the theme of the book and its implications. What are the theological implications here, and implications for Church practice including the training of clergy or lay leaders? What are the ecumenical and interfaith possibilities? Finally, there is the possibility of an eco-Church model for Australia.

Definitions

In order to add a degree of precision, it is important at the outset to attempt to define a number of words which are used throughout this book.

Theology is of course basic, and as such is probably understood at least in general terms; but Macquarrie's definition may be regarded as an adequate starting point: "Theology may be defined as the study which, through participation in and reflection upon a religious faith, seeks to express the content of this faith in the clearest and most cogent language available"[3]. Beyond that, it is usual to speak of particular branches of theology; in that context, **eco-theology** is a recognised descriptor of an approach that sets theology in dialogue with contemporary ecology, and asserts that our care of the natural world, or of God's creation, is not just a practical issue, but a faith issue as well. Thus, it does not in any way set out to deny or diminish the traditional and legitimate issues that theology addresses; it is simply a term of convenience to identify a particular aspect of that theology.

Mission is another significant word that needs an explanation, although it may be noted that books on that subject frequently fail to offer a definition, apparently assuming that its meaning is self-explanatory. Perhaps Bosch is correct in suggesting that "mission" is ultimately indefinable. However, although chapter 7 will be devoted to an exploration of the term, especially in its ecological implications, a brief interim explanation may be attempted. In basic terms, I take it to refer to the role of the Christian Church in the world in its wholeness, including worship and spiritual disciplines, pastoral care and a compassionate response to human need, in addition to social justice and ecological issues as suggested by Jesus' use of the term "kingdom

---

3 John Macquarrie. 1977. *Principles of Christian Theology* (Revised Edition). (London: SCM Press), 1.

of God". In short, as Bosch states, "mission gives expression to the dynamic relationship between God and the world"[4].

But as in the case of theology and eco-theology, **eco-mission** builds on the foundation of eco-theology to express the conviction that Christians are called to safeguard the integrity of creation, and to exercise their mission in such a way that the life of the Earth is sustained and renewed. As such it operates alongside other valid forms of Christian mission; it makes no claim to be the whole of mission, but it has its part to play in an ecclesiastical ethos that has often overlooked this dimension.

There are four different words commonly used to describe the natural world. These are nature, environment, ecology, and creation, and while they are often used more or less interchangeably, there are some subtle differences to be noted.

Nature is probably one of the more commonly used descriptors of non-human life, and most of us probably assume that we know what it means. A typical definition is that it refers to "the physical world, including plants, animals, the landscape, and natural phenomena, as opposed to people or things made by people"[5]. It is of course broader than that, and includes the essential qualities of a person or thing. But in general terms it is taken to refer to the largely untamed countryside.

Nature is understood by some to include a scientific study of plant and animal life, and to reflect the assumption of a different relationship between humans and the ecological system. That "different relationship" is often assumed to be one of dominance rather than partnership. However, James Nash illustrates the danger of assuming that the meaning of a word is self-evident when he defines nature as "simply the biospherical world, *of which humans are parts and products*" (italics mine)[6]. The question of whether humans are part of nature has important implications in terms of the attitudes we bring to it, and I will therefore be arguing that Nash is correct

---

4 David J. Bosch, 1991. *Transforming Mission: Paradigm Shifts in Theology of Mission.* (Maryknoll, NY: Orbis Books), 9.

5 C Soanes and S Hawker. *Compact Oxford English Dictionary of Current English.* 3rd edition revised. (Oxford: Oxford University Press, 2008), 677.

6 James Nash, *Loving Nature: Ecological Integrity and Christian Responsibility.* (Nashville: Abingdon, 1991), 22.

in his assessment. To see ourselves as separate from nature is to invite an increased likelihood of abuse.

Environment includes the whole context in which life is lived. Thus, environment would include not only the ecological system, but also the buildings that we create, the social structure of society, and all that is implied in the phrase "the political and scientific aspect of the whole"[7]. In theological terms that is significant, in that the presence and action of God may be perceived in the whole human context. James Nash has a concern that "environment" carries a human-centred or anthropocentric connotation, and relates primarily to the human context. That concern must be noted, and certainly a human dimension is involved, but whether that is primary is another question.

Ecology may at first seem little different from a more general concept such as nature, and certainly definitions vary in their scope. It may be understood in the narrowly scientific terms of non-human organisms in relationship with their environment. G Tyler Miller describes ecology as "a study of organisms in their home; it is a study of the structure and function of nature or of the organisms and groups of organisms found in nature and their interactions with one another and with their environment"[8]; in other words, the ecological ideal is the pursuit of a complete understanding of the entire ecosphere. Such an understanding provides the context for a more complete approach; while it may appear at first that ecology has little to do with humankind, in fact that would be quite deceptive.

The Webster's Dictionary definition cited by Carmody[9] also includes community issues and social interaction. More than that, Carmody calls on Tyler Miller's analysis of the scientific and sociological aspects of ecology. In that analysis Miller uses the laws of thermodynamics to illustrate the need for environmental sustainability. That in turn illustrates the impossibility of defining ecology adequately without reference to humankind.

Thus, ecology speaks of a network of relationships between different life forms, in a natural non-political setting. Santmire sums it up well when

7 Ulrich Duchrow & Gerhard Liedke. *Shalom: Biblical Perspectives on Creation, Justice, and Peace* (Geneva: WCC Publications, 1989), 49.
8 G Tyler Miller. *Living in the Environment.* (Belmont, CA: Wadsworth, 1982), 44.
9 John Carmody. *Ecology and Religion: Toward a New Christian Theology of Nature.* (New York: Paulist Press, 1983).

he states that ecology is "a network of interrelationships between God, humanity, and nature"[10]. This can be taken at a global, regional, or local level. Every rainforest, for example, has its own particular eco-system, set within the larger network of global ecology. But it is also possible to draw on more general nuances of the word. Ruether relates ecology to biological science, describing it as "the biological science of biotic communities that demonstrates the laws by which nature, unaided by humans, has generated and sustained life"[11].

Creation introduces a broader and deeper dimension to our understanding, and includes not only what we understand as ecology or nature, but also the universe itself. The key is the faith or belief that God created matter and is the source of life, and this is God's world. Thus, it is not merely the belief that God "made everything", but also that God alone is the basis of meaning and value in all things. As Moltmann states, "The limited sphere of reality which we call 'nature' must be lifted into the totality of being which is termed 'God's creation'"[12], and that inevitably includes an element of relationship with God. It cannot be extended to mean that all societal systems, for example, are God's creation, but rather that all things are subject to divine authority. The concept of creation therefore, as an ongoing process, adds a new and deeper dimension to the current concern about the future of the planet. What will it mean to be answerable not just to our peers or even our children and grandchildren, but to our God for the quality of our stewardship?

Limitations

It will be apparent that the broad theme of ecology and Christian mission potentially offers enormous scope, and thus some boundaries need to be set.

First, it is beyond the scope of this book to undertake a comprehensive theology of the environment, but rather it must content itself with a summary approach that is able to support a theology of ecological mission. Moreover, it means that we will be dealing more with general principles

---

10 H Paul Santmire. *The Travail of Nature – the Ambiguous Ecological Promise of Christian Theology.* (Minneapolis, MN: Fortress Press, 1985), 9.
11 Rosemary Radford Ruether. *Gaia and God: an ecofeminist theology of earth healing.* (San Francisco: HarperSanFrancisco, 1992), 47.
12 J Moltmann. *God in Creation: An Ecological Doctrine of Creation.* (London: SCM Press Ltd, 1985), 21.

rather than the exploration of particular programs or details concerning the way those principles may be applied. Local circumstances will vary widely; but in any event I believe that this work will facilitate the formulation of specific eco-mission plans and strategies.

Second, while I have already drawn attention to some of the scientific underpinnings of ecological concern, this book should not in any sense be viewed as a quasi-scientific exercise. As I have suggested, a degree of consensus is emerging in the scientific community, and while a summary of some key issues is helpful in understanding the current concern and urgency, it is nonetheless not a central component of the book. Further, I am not qualified to express scientific opinions; the main focus of the work is theological.

Third, while this book must of necessity focus on a Christian perspective, it is important to acknowledge the enormous scope and potential for an inter-faith approach to ecological issues. This is reflected for example in *Earth and Faith: a Book of Reflection and Action* published by the United Nations in 2000. Further, there is significant variation within the Christian community itself, and while those differences would offer some fascinating material, my aim here is to do the basic theology and see where it takes us.

Conclusion

This is potentially a large subject with many facets, but with the imposition of some essential limitations, it is my hope that it will represent a positive contribution.

CHAPTER TWO

Context and Approach

There are many contextual issues for Christian mission in Australia; these would include the decline of faith in Australia, huge physical and ethical issues and needs, changed value systems and philosophies, and other world faiths. But there is one critical contextual issue that will be our focus here, and that is a multi-dimensional environmental crisis, which in turn is clearly related to many social justice issues.

In the first chapter I referred to the seriousness of the ecological crisis, as in global warming and other disastrous outcomes that many believe we have brought upon ourselves. In this chapter I want to elaborate on that theme; but I want to go further than that to consider the wider contextual issue of how much may be included under the heading of the term "eco-crisis". In short, what is the scope of the crisis?

At the outset it may appear that "eco-crisis" is an accurate enough description of an increasingly obvious global reality. On closer examination, however, it will appear to be a term that is seriously limiting in its grasp. As James Nash states, to talk of the "environmental problem" is rather like referring to a nuclear conflagration as a fire. Thus he asserts that it is not "a single, discrete problem, but rather a massive mosaic of intertwined problems" adversely affecting all life[1]. That assessment is demonstrably correct, as also is his perception that the issues involved are primarily of a moral nature.

In a similar vein, Moltmann argues that "the natural environment of human beings cannot be understood apart from the social environment", and asserts that what we face is really "a crisis of the whole life system of the modern industrial world"[2]. The point not only for Moltmann but also for Nash and others is that humans have created the crisis we are now experiencing, and we are "going in more deeply". Since powerful forces are at work in this process, the economic and social conditions of human life must be changed for the sake of our ecological future. I contend that

---

1 James Nash. *Loving Nature*, 23.
2 Moltmann. *God in Creation*, 23.

this wider perspective of the crisis is helpful in understanding the current situation and how to respond to it.

Duchrow and Liedke point to an additional perspective in the way we approach the crisis. Our point of departure, they contend, can no longer be the goodness of creation, but rather it can only be the suffering of creation. They go on to observe that "the presupposition for the understanding of the ecological crisis as creation's suffering is the suspension of the sharp division between human beings and nature"[3]. That of course raises other issues that will be considered later, such as Hart's contention that justice for people and for the environment are inseparable, and that humans exist "in an interrelated and inter-dependent biosphere and universe"[4]. Thus, in this book, while the term "eco-crisis" may still be used, it will be as a kind of shorthand for the broader context I have outlined here.

There is one other important introductory observation to be made, and that is the obvious point that this book is not a scientific study; for reliable and up to date climate science information the reader should refer to some of the official reports that are released from time to time[5]. In any event there is a sense in which the clear scientific evidence has little bearing on my central argument, which is theologically based. Nevertheless, for the sake of completeness it is essential to include some indication of an emerging scientific consensus in a number of crucial environmental areas. This will obviously not be complete, since the subject is large, complex, and constantly changing; rather, its purpose will largely be illustrative and indicative of a huge problem for planet Earth and for life as we know it. It certainly adds a sense of urgency to the moral, ethical, and theological challenge facing not only the Church, but also indeed all humankind in these days.

The Global Ecology

The scope of the crisis is revealed in the first instance through a study of the global ecological context. There are many ways in which that may be illustrated, but I will focus largely, although not exclusively, on the issue

---

3 Duchrow and Liedke. *Shalom*, 50.

4 John Hart. *What are They Saying about Environmental Theology?* (Mahwah, New Jersey: Paulist Press, 2004), 4.

5 See for example W Steffen and L Hughes, *The Critical Decade 2013: Climate Change Science, Risks and Responses* (Commonwealth of Australia, 2013).

of climate change and global warming, which in itself introduces a whole range of significant implications, such as the possibility of mass extinctions and a loss of bio-diversity.

One of the earliest threats to life globally was that posed by stratospheric ozone depletion which was spelled out in the Scientists' Warning to the United Nations in 1992. Flannery traces the depletion of the ozone layer in the last half of the 20th century: "By 2000 the hole had become a chasm spanning 28 million square kilometres, and around it had spread a halo of thinned ozone covering most of the globe below 40 degrees South.... Even over the tropics, ozone concentration was reduced by around 7 per cent". He goes on to state that "without ozone's very high sun-protection factor, ultraviolet radiation would kill you fast"[6]. Clearly, such a level of ozone depletion would have serious health and other implications not only for humankind, but also for many life forms. Moreover, before the ozone layer had formed early in the evolutionary process, life on earth was not possible; if it is destroyed through human stupidity and greed, life will again become impossible. It is a question of existence itself. The good news, however, is that there is some evidence that this process of destruction may be in the early stages of recovery, because of remedial actions that have been taken. The question is whether there will be any good news emerging over climate change!

Global Warning and Scepticism

For some years now, scientists have been sounding a warning about the environment, as in the case of the famous "Doomsday Alert" presented to the United Nations General Assembly in 1992 by 1,575 scientists, including many Nobel Prize winners. Scientists have clearly been exercising what could only be described as a prophetic role regarding the environment; and, just as in the days of the Hebrew prophets, there have been many who have not believed their message, although that situation has been changing.

Yet "enviro-scepticism" is still a phenomenon, and reservations remain in the minds of some people. Certainly there are scientists who are sceptical about the notion of human-induced climate change, although they are a minority[7] and certainly do not include many *climate* scientists. John

6 Tim Flannery, *The Weather Makers: The History and Future Impact of Climate Change*. (Melbourne: Text Publishing, 2005), 215-6.

7 A prominent example of that minority view is Singer and Avery's *Unstoppable Climate Change*, which purports to show that global warming is a natural event that occurs every 1,500 years.

Cook and some colleagues have analysed nearly 12,000 climate abstracts from 1991 to 2011 and found that of the abstracts which expressed a view about anthropogenic global warming, over 97% endorsed the consensus. Moreover, contrary to some public perception and statements in the media, the consensus is increasing while papers rejecting the consensus are "a vanishingly small proportion" of the published work[8]. Among ordinary people as well there can be a temptation to believe what we want to believe, and we should all beware the approach or response that is ideologically driven. On the other hand, as Dupont and Pearman suggest in their Lowy Institute Report, scepticism has played an important role in that it has led to "better science and therefore greater certainty about the scope, magnitude and implications of climate change"[9].

The political arena is another complicating factor, and the politicising of the important climate situation easily leads to "red herrings" and a *de facto* compromising of important data. When myths are paraded as facts it can be very confusing for the community at large which needs to be discerning in these matters. But in any event, and in spite of the sceptics, there is an increasing consensus in the scientific community about the weight of evidence for both climate change and its human causes.

Climate Change and its Implications

If climatology is still "an inexact science", as Nash[10] suggests, it should be noted it has progressed considerably in the years since 1991. It represents a mature and reliable discipline that for the past several decades at least has been presenting a consistent report of global climate. A number of significant Reports over the past decade all tell a similar story. As the Stern Report states, "The scientific evidence is now overwhelming: climate change presents very serious global risks, and it demands an urgent global response"[11], and the passage of time has only strengthened that case.

---

8 J. Cook, D. Nuccitelli, S.A. Green, M. Richardson, B. Winkler, R. Painting, R. Way, P. Jacobs, & A. Skuce. (2013). Quantifying the consensus on anthropogenic global warming in the scientific literature. *Environmental Research Letters*, 8(2), 024024+.

9 Dupont and Pearman *Heating*, 25.

10 Nash. *Loving Nature*, 34.

11 Nicholas Stern, *The Stern Review: The Economics of Climate Change (Executive Summary.)* (www.hm-treasury.gov.uk 2006), 1.

In my home State of Queensland, the Government issued a significant discussion paper on climate change in 2005 which stated bluntly, "Queensland is getting hotter, and our temperatures are rising more rapidly than both the global and national averages"[12]. It goes on to note changes in the rainfall patterns, the increased intensity of storms, and likely shortages of water. Important though that was, it did not make many headlines. But public perception of environmental matters began to change noticeably during 2006, urged on by a number of factors. One was the publicity given to Al Gore's film "An Inconvenient Truth", and the Stern Report in Britain; the comprehensive Report by the Lowy Institute, *Heating Up the Planet*, which sought to bring together the scientific consensus about global warming, appeared to make a relatively minor impact.

In a more immediate sense, by the end of that year it was increasingly obvious that something significant was happening to the climate. In many parts of Australia, a prolonged drought was causing grave concern, and it began to affect much more than the rural sector. Cities and towns accustomed to taking water for granted suddenly faced a crisis. This led to dramatic newspaper headlines such as "We could run out of water", or "Australia suffers worst drought in 1,000 years". Severe water restrictions had to be imposed, and some towns even ran out of water. The sequel in 2011 was widespread devastating flooding which created enormous damage, but by 2013 much of the State was again in drought and records are constantly being broken. All of that is in addition to other areas of major concern such as the huge Murray-Darling system. It is of course true that Australia has always experienced drought and flooding; the difference now is in the intensity and frequency of those events. In recent years climate has become news on a regular basis, and formerly apathetic or sceptical politicians can no longer ignore it, even if they do not always treat it with the seriousness it deserves.

The Intergovernmental Panel on Climate Change (IPCC), chaired by Sir John Houghton for some years, issued a Report in 2006, called "Global Warming, Climate Change, and Sustainability", which indicated that the global average temperature is predicted to rise by between 2 and 6 degrees Celsius from its pre-industrial level. But a number of factors must be kept

---

12 Queensland Government. 2005. *Climate Smart: What does Climate Change Mean for You?* Page 1.

in mind. First, these are *average* figures, so that there may be variation either up or down, and in addition there will of course be considerable regional variation. Data since 2006 suggests that it is going to be a challenge to keep the projected increase at the low end of the range. Clive Hamilton[13] quotes the IEA[14] position that if governments do no more than institute current policies, the world will warm by 3.5% by the end of the century; if those modest targets are not met, the figure could be at the high end of the projection. Either way it would represent a rather different world from the one we have known. Second, as the 2013 Report of the Climate Commission in Australia notes, "a small increase in average temperature can have a surprisingly large effect on the number of hot days and record hot days"[15]. Third, such an increase in temperature will have a number of flow-on effects which will exacerbate the global situation.

The drastic nature of these forecasts is exacerbated by the short timeframe in which change is taking place. As sceptics are usually quick to point out, there has always been variation in the earth's temperature. This is something else again, and it relates to both the extent and pace of change. Speaking out of his background in climatology, Houghton states, "So, associated with likely warming in the 21st century will be a rate of change equivalent to say, half an ice age in less than 100 years – a larger rate of change than for at least 10,000 years. Adapting to this will be difficult for both humans and many ecosystems"[16]. Put another way, since the peak of the last Ice Age about 18,000 years ago, the earth's average temperature has warmed by only about 5 degrees centigrade[17].

The IPCC Summary Report in February 2007 stated that "Warming of the climate system is unequivocal", and goes on to indicate that "Most of the observed increase in globally averaged temperature since the mid-20th century is very likely (>90% probability) due to the observed increase in

---

13 Clive Hamilton, *Earth Masters: Playing God with the Climate.* (Crows Nest, NSW: Allen and Unwin, 2013).
14 International Energy Agency of the OECD.
15 Will Steffen and Lesley Hughes. *The Critical Decade 2013: Climate Change Science, Risks and Responses,* (Climate Commission Secretariat, Commonwealth of Australia, 2013), 54.
16 John Houghton, *Global Warming, Climate Change and Sustainability: Challenge to Scientists, Policy Makers, and Christians.* Cheltenham (UK: John Ray Initiative, 2007 (i). (Briefing Paper 14), 4.
17 Nash. *Loving Nature,* 33.

anthropogenic greenhouse gas concentrations"[18]. The IPCC Report in 2013 has increased the likelihood of climate change having a human cause to 95%, which leaves little room for doubt. Or as the Lowy Institute Report asserts, the evidence implicating humans as the cause of the problem is now "irrefutable"[19]. Moreover, as Dupont and Pearman go on to suggest, "while a great deal of the data is no longer in dispute, most people do not have a realistic sense of the magnitude of likely future climate change because scientists have largely failed to communicate the significance of their findings in a way that policy makers, the media, and the general public can easily understand"[20].

Until its dismantling in 2013, the Climate Commission in Australia brought together internationally recognised climate scientists, policy and business leaders; fortunately the Commission members took immediate action to re-launch the group as an independent Climate Council with significant public support. In 2011 the Commission stated that the decade 2011-2020 is "the critical decade" – "the decade to decisively begin the journey to decarbonise our economy, thereby reducing the risks posed by climate change"[21]. The Report is too significant to attempt to summarise in a paragraph, but its key findings include the following:

1. Understanding of the climate system continues to strengthen.

2. Social, economic, and environmental consequences of climate change are evident and expressed in heatwaves, bushfires, rainfall patterns, and sea-level rises.

3. The changes pose serious risks for health, property, infrastructure, agriculture, and eco-systems.

4. While some progress has been made globally, far more will be needed.

5. "It is clear that most fossil fuels must be left in the ground and cannot be burned"[22].

---

18 John Houghton, *IPCC Fourth Assessment Report (FAR), Summary for Policymakers*. John Ray Initiative website, 2007 (ii).
19 Dupont and Pearman, *Heating*, 10
20 Dupont and Pearman, *Heating*, 25
21 Climate Commission Report, 3.
22 Climate Commission Report, 4, 5.

This is in keeping with the assertion of Stanford climate scientists Diffenbaugh and Field that climate change is on track to occur at a rate 10 times faster than at any time in the last 65 million years, a pace which "could lead to a 5-degree Celsius spike in annual temperature by the end of the century". In other words, this 2013 Report is completely consistent with the earlier material, and in fact the problems are compounding. Quite clearly, the implications of global warming have a considerable flow-on effect.

Sea ice in both of the Polar Regions is melting at a rate that alarms many scientists; the North West Passage, for example, is open as never before. The IPCC Report indicates that "the last time the Polar Regions were significantly warmer than at present for an extended period (about 125,000 years ago), reductions in polar ice volumes led to 4 to 6 metres of sea level rise"[23]. It will of course take some years for any dramatic rises to become evident, but it should be noted that some low lying areas of the Pacific, for example, are already experiencing difficulties and have begun to make their voices heard. Stern indicates that "more than a fifth of Bangladesh could be under water with a 1m rise in sea levels, which is a possibility by the end of the century"[24]. The flow of fresh water into the ocean from melted Arctic ice in areas such as Greenland is expected to have a devastating impact on the flow of the warm Gulf Stream; if the Gulf Stream were to slow down or to stop altogether, a British winter could ironically resemble a mini Ice Age. Gore also discusses that possibility, and reflects serious scientific concern that such a phenomenon, which occurred about 10,000 years ago, could recur in the modern era. The melting of Himalayan ice could place perhaps one-sixth of the world's population, who depend on the rivers sourced there, in jeopardy.

Food production will be significantly impacted by global warming, and Dupont and Pearman point to four ways in which that will happen. First, seed sterility in some cereal, pasture, and tree species will increase. Agricultural research indicates that food production in Asia could decrease by up to 20% if rises are in the predicted range. Second, changing patterns of rainfall "could render previously productive land infertile, accelerating

---

23 Houghton. *Fourth Assessment Report.*
24 Stern, *Review,* vii.

erosion, desertification, and reducing crop and livestock yields"[25]. A loss of irrigation water could be devastating, especially in Australia and Asia. Third, as sea levels rise, some highly productive coastal land will become unusable. Fish species are already starting to migrate to other waters, while coral bleaching has led to concern about the future of the iconic Great Barrier Reef. Fourth, extreme weather events, such as cyclones, will increase, and as evidenced in North Queensland in 2006, will seriously disrupt agricultural production. There is evidence that extreme events have already begun; for example, 2005 was a record year for Atlantic hurricanes and typhoons, both in their number and intensity.

Climate change will have a serious impact on health globally. Dupont and Pearman warn that beyond global warming, the resulting extreme weather events, air pollution, water diseases, vector and rodent borne diseases, and food and water shortages will lead to illness and death. Stern points to an increased problem with diseases such as malaria and dengue fever, as well as heat stress, to which may be added, in some cases, problems with extreme cold.

The 2013 IPCC Report has confirmed the mounting evidence that natural disasters are increasing in severity in line with the warming of the planet. As the Lowy Report suggests, there may be other factors at work also, but the insurance industry is of the view that there is a connection. The Report indicates that of the last 20 major insurance events in Australia, 19 have been weather related. So far as cyclones are concerned, the severity is expected to be more intense even if frequency remains constant. That of course also has significant social and economic implications, and puts a much greater burden on aid and relief organizations, including Church-based groups. Significantly changed rainfall patterns will exacerbate the situation and have important flow-on effects.

To add to the burden, with problems in such areas as food production, health issues, water shortages and flooding, the projected rise in sea levels as the century progresses could well lead to massive numbers of environmental refugees, with the greatest impact being on the poorer peoples of the world. Houghton states, "A careful estimate has suggested that, due to climate change, there could be more than 150 million extra

---

25 Dupont and Pearman, *Heating*, 30-31.

refugees by 2050"[26]. From an Australian perspective that becomes a real and present issue as low lying Pacific nations such as Tuvalu or Kiribati are increasingly threatened by the sea. When the ocean starts to swallow the land, the people need somewhere to go, and a high degree of uncertainty and nervousness about the future is understandable. Thus, as Dupont and Pearman note in the Lowy Report, security emerges as a significant focus for the climate future that is threatening. The dynamics of international relations could be affected in a dramatic and unpredictable way.

There is more to it even than that, because the Earth consists of vast inter-locking eco-systems. Thus it is all life, and not just humanity, that is at risk here. In line with the 1992 Warning to the U.N., Stern indicates that a rise of only two degrees Celsius would lead to the extinction of between 15 and 40% of species. There is considerable evidence that climate change is one of the factors involved in a process of species loss is already taking place. In March 2006, ABC News Online cited a Report of the UN Convention on Biological Diversity: "In effect, we are currently responsible for the sixth major extinction event in the history of earth, and the greatest since the dinosaurs disappeared, 65 million years ago"; but more than that, this is the only one for which humans are primarily responsible, and the current pace of extinctions is estimated to be 1,000 times faster than historical rates.

Such a loss of biodiversity of both plant and animal life is an ecological issue of considerable significance, even when viewed from a purely human perspective. The comprehensive United Nations report known as GEO-4 contains an enormous amount of material that cannot be covered here; but the authors assert the fundamental role of biodiversity as "the basis for ecosystems and the services they provide, upon which all people fundamentally depend"[27]. Such a dependency is spelled out in terms of health, future development options, agriculture, livelihood security, as well as cultural and spiritual identity. The loss of biodiversity due in large part to economically dominated policies is therefore far more than merely inconvenient; the effect on wildlife and on human life alike is profound, and inevitably in the human community it is the poor who pay the highest price.

---

26 Houghton, *Global Warming*, 5.
27 United Nations Environment Program. *Global Environmental Outlook GEO4, 190.*

The term "Anthropocene" was popularised by the atmospheric chemist Paul Crutzen as an emerging but apt descriptor of the current geological epoch in which it is widely recognised that human impact steers the environment. This would be given added credence if, as Hamilton documents, governments embark on the dangerous path of what is called geoengineering. What that means is that we forget about trying to live sustainably and instead engineer the climate using high risk grand scale technological interventions; that really would be "playing God with the climate"[28].

More than Ecology is Involved

I have described some of the diverse implications of climate change and global warming, but there are many other ways of describing what is loosely called the eco-crisis. Data on a number of issues, such as energy use and waste, population growth, excessive consumption, pollution, desertification, acidification, and much more, has been accumulating for some years now, and examples are almost endless. Even this brief ecological survey is a clear demonstration that in most respects the crisis is a consequence of human activity, and that a much wider agenda is also involved. Consequently it is impossible to talk about ecological issues without taking into account the broader dimensions of human life and activity.

Proponents of several different but related schools of thought unite to affirm the broader context of the eco-crisis. A full exposition of their approaches is not necessary here, but some basic points may be noted. The eco-justice school, for example, broadly speaking sits at the junction of ecology, justice, and theology. Not surprisingly, it may also include a political dimension, which in some cases is quite striking. A prime example is the Brazilian, Leonardo Boff, whose 1995 work, *Ecology and Liberation: A New Paradigm,* brings together both ecology and justice with spirituality and theology. He calls on the Church to "find loudspeakers that will allow (the voice of the poor) to be heard effectively"[29]. His primary motivation, I believe, is revealed in his observation that "the dream is not of either a poor society or a rich one, but one of a just and sharing life for the whole of creation".

Others, such as Sean McDonagh, are less overtly political. McDonagh served as a Catholic missionary to the T'boli people of the Philippines, and

---

28 See Clive Hamilton, *Earth Masters.*
29 L. Boff *Ecology and Liberation: a New Paradigm.* (Maryknoll, NY: Orbis Books, 1995), 108.

that has largely shaped his understanding of the close connection between culture, justice, and ecology. He refers to Church documents such as *Populorum Progressio,* from which he cites the Apostolic Letter to Cardinal Roy, for example, and states: "These documents insist that the poverty which is affecting more and more of the world's population is directly related to the misuse and squandering of natural and human resources in first-world, mostly traditional Christian countries"[30]. But he argues that countries in the developing world also are partly to blame, through incompetence, corruption, useless projects, and huge foreign debts. Thus, "We can no longer take the natural world for granted as if it will always be there unchanged"[31].

Beyond the boundaries of a particular school of thought, it is now generally acknowledged that there is a widening gap between the rich and the poor, both within and across national borders; this serious disparity shows that the rich end of the human spectrum consumes far more, and the poorer end far less, than their entitlement. But more than that, as the Stern Report states in relation to climate change, the impacts are not evenly distributed; "the poorest countries and people will suffer earliest and most"[32].

The blunt fact is that the world could not even begin to sustain an overall consumption rate at the level of the wealthier nations; there is only one Earth. In other words, we are not living in a way that is sustainable, and at the risk of over-simplification, some are poor because others are rich. The claim that famine is caused primarily through poor distribution may not be as simple as it sounds; certainly there is a huge amount of food wastage in the developed world. A report titled "State of Food Insecurity in the World 2012"[33], published jointly by the United Nations Food and Agriculture Organization, the International Fund for Agricultural Development and the World Food Program estimated that almost 870 million people are under-nourished; the vast majority are in developing countries, but 15 million are in developed countries. It also indicates that global progress in reducing hunger has slowed.

---

30 Sean McDonagh, *Passion for the Earth: the Christian Vocation to Promote Justice, Peace, and the Integrity of Creation.* (London: Geoffrey Chapman, 1994), p.5.
31 McDonagh, *Passion,* 9.
32 *Stern Report,* vii.
33 http://www.fao.org/news/story

It is noteworthy that the World Council of Churches' important work in the environmental area is organised by the Justice, Peace, and the Integrity of Creation Commission, otherwise known as JPIC. From that perspective, there are other issues that should be included in any discussion of the eco-crisis. Potentially it opens up some very large subjects that cannot be canvassed here. But, for example, at any one time there are numerous conflicts of one kind or another throughout the world, some of which have their roots in inter-religious tensions; and when those conflicts are added to the current ecological situation, the wastage in human, non-human, and environmental terms is incalculable. Ultimately everything is connected, and has a bearing on God's good creation and the sustainability of life within it.

Thus, it starts to become obvious that the current crisis does not exist independently of either national boundaries or the human community. In his report on the Stockholm Earth Summit, Granberg-Michaelson states that debate focussed on "the suspicion that environmental concerns are a luxury of affluent Northern societies"[34]. At the Rio Summit, however, there was the perception that this was more than just a regional or national matter. Whether it related to the use of CFCs, the environmental impact of poverty, extreme weather events, or something else, "ecology has been seen in its global dimension"[35]. Granberg-Michaelson's words may seem dramatic, but they are as true today as they were in 1992:

> The point is that in the two decades between Stockholm and the Earth Summit in Rio de Janeiro, evidence became overwhelming that ecological damage is global in nature, binding North and South together towards an escalating common tragedy, or on new paths towards a common, sustainable future[36].

In this book therefore I want to acknowledge fully both the great complexity and the wide scope of the crisis confronting all life on the planet. As I have argued, ecology cannot ultimately be considered in isolation. However, because until comparatively recent times ecology has tended to be overlooked in theological deliberations and in public consideration of the issues, it is my intention to focus on that aspect.

---

34 Wesley Granberg-Michaelson, *Redeeming the Creation.* (Geneva: WCC Publications, 1992), p.9.
35 Granberg-Michaelson, *Redeeming,* 11.
36 Granberg-Michaelson, *Redeeming,* 17.

The Church in the Eco Crisis

What then is the role of the Christian Church in this crisis? In many instances it has not been involved in it, although there is a rapidly growing list of exceptions to that judgment. Some Church jurisdictions, confessional bodies and ecumenical bodies have made statements, while the volume of academic literature on eco-theology has certainly escalated in recent decades. Without making excuses, there are probably a number of factors at work. As I will argue, part of the problem is the volume of highly anthropocentric or human-centred theology in the past; in fact one of the issues that will be addressed is the charge that theology is largely to blame for the crisis. Further, there has often been an assumption that Christian mission is essentially focussed on human issues, or even simply "winning people for Christ". Further, it must be said that until quite recently the eco-crisis has largely been the preserve of a minority working through various environmental groups.

Thus, there are three background issues in this matter of creation care, namely an emerging consensus in the scientific community, an increasing volume of eco-theological material, and the development of a theology of Christian mission that includes eco-mission. It is the seriousness of the global eco-crisis that adds a sense of purpose and urgency to the question of the Church's role. At the same time, the task of saving the planet from the excesses of its human population is by no means the task of the Christian Church alone. A response must come from all levels, including environmental groups, business, government, and the population at large. Rising out of those two issues, therefore, and building on the firm principles of a sound ecotheology, it is my contention that ecological issues must be on the Church's agenda at all levels – both denominationally and ecumenically, at regional, state and national levels, in theological education, and in local congregations.

If the Church's basic theology fails to take sufficient account of the biosphere as creation, it is unlikely to be aware of a range of legitimate implications. Further, while a theology of Christian eco-mission can emerge from a number of different theological positions, eco-mission nevertheless relates strongly to eco-theology. This is most evident, for example, in the notion of stewardship of the Earth, a stance that clearly rises out of the theology, and which in turn becomes a key point of an eco-mission theology. Such a theology poses serious questions for the practical mission of the Church that need to be addressed. In short, how can practical action in and through the Church on behalf of the environment be more effective?

One problem is that while there is an increasing volume of literature on eco-theology covering many different facets of the subject, there is relatively little relating to the mission side of the issue, especially at a practical level in Australia. But practical action is bedded in the theology. My tasks in this book are therefore to bring the crisis and the Church together, clarify the theological underpinnings of the issue, to help the Christian community to understand its ecological role, and to discover ways in which it can contribute, alongside other groups, in alleviating and hopefully beginning to reverse the crisis facing the planet, for the good not only of humankind, but also indeed of all life.

One assumption I am making is that the situation can be changed, and for two essential reasons. First, community concern about the environment is clearly rising. This is reflected, for example, in opinion polls and media exposure regarding global warming. It has become a major political issue, at least in the sense that it cannot be ignored. For pragmatic reasons even if not for theological ones, the Church will not be able to ignore this issue; and it has to be said, there are many who do not want to ignore it. But second, my hope is that as the Christian community begins to come to terms with eco-theology and a consequent theology of eco-mission, many will come to embrace what I believe is the correct biblical and theological stance with regard to life, and our home, the Earth.

Possible Variation

It is true in a very general sense that positive action on behalf of the environment may emerge out of a range of quite different positions, both theistic and atheistic. However, the focus of this book is the Christian Church; and within the Church the undergirding theology becomes very important. What Christians believe about God, the Church and the world in theological terms will tend to shape their theology of mission, and that in turn will largely determine the nature of their mission within human communities.

Thus, a Church that focuses on the imminent return of Christ, that believes this world is coming to an end, or believes that the most critical issue for the Church is to seek people's commitment to Christ in order to ensure their bliss in an after-life, is not likely to be strongly motivated to care for the Earth. The challenge facing such Christians is to be open to the demonstration that eco-mission is firmly rooted in the Bible. Moreover, when theology perceives that God not only created the world and called it "good" (Gen 1), but also that God is immanent in the world, then the divine call to "tend the Earth and keep it" (Gen 2:15) will find a deeper resonance.

Once an eco-friendly theological stance has been adopted, it is not essential or even appropriate to insist on a particular "correct" position regarding broader theological issues. Like most others, I have a preferred theological position, and it is one that I consider is conducive to positive ecological outcomes; however, within the confines I have outlined, effective ecological mission is able to emerge from differing theological positions.

The Assumptions we make

The discipline of hermeneutics is based on a Greek word that means "to announce", or to "translate" or "interpret". It has traditionally been understood as relating to the interpretation of texts, especially the texts of Scripture, although it is of course wider than that, and may include discourse and action. We do not need to delve into that here, but it does raise a very important question. How do we deal with the assumptions we inevitably bring to the text or event?

Many of us would have to acknowledge an assumption that the Christian Faith is essentially about humankind – how we should live and what our final destiny might be. The assumptions we bring to any text will inevitably colour the understanding we draw from that text. So it is with the Bible. But what if that assumption is wrong? Perhaps at this point it may be appropriate to refer to the role of imagination and "a hermeneutic of suspicion"; in particular Habel's use of this notion in terms of an ecological reading of the Scriptures is significant. Habel observes that "The Bible has long been understood as God's book for humans"[37], and there is no problem with that so long as we do not impose limitations on the text. Habel's "Earth Bible" team consciously avoided the assumption that the *exclusive* focus of the Biblical message is humanity, and sought "to focus on Earth itself as the

---

37 Norman Habel, *Readings from the Perspective of Earth.* Sheffield: Sheffield Academic Press, 2000), 39

object of investigation in the text"[38]; far from being negative, the "suspicion" enables the text to be heard in a fresh way and results in a whole new level of understanding.

A positive approach would perceive that what is required is, as Gadamer states, "… to be aware of one's own bias, so that the text may present itself in all its newness and thus be able to assert its own truth…[39]". More than that, as Farley suggests, the interpretation of texts and situations from the viewpoint and in the context of faith creates "a specific hermeneutic task"; and the first task, he suggests, is in identifying and describing the situation[40]. Yet I cannot undertake that task outside the faith perspective I bring to it. More than that, there is a range of philosophical, scientific, and theological responses that need to be taken into account, along with the very practical matter of the Church's response to the crisis. It is in such a setting that a practical theology model becomes most appropriate.

A Practical Theology Model

The nature of the crisis we face suggests strongly that a practical theology represents the most appropriate paradigm; how should it be defined? For Farley, practical theology is that dimension of theology "in which reflection is directed at a living situation in which the believer or corporate entity is involved"[41]. Ogletree offers what I believe is a helpful comment. "Theology is practical in the sense that it concerns, in all of its expressions, the most basic issues of human existence"[42]. It does have its theoretical side, he argues, in which we need to stand back from a particular experience in order to understand more clearly what is happening around us. But that is not an end in itself.

Forrester's observation is also compelling; while emphasising that practical theology is *theology*, he asserts that we cannot talk about God or talk to God while setting aside, even temporarily, the ethical or normative question:

---

38 Habel, *Readings*, 38

39 Hans-Georg Gadamer, 1979. *Truth and Method*. (London: Sheed and Ward, 1979), 236

40 E Farley, *Interpreting Situations: An Inquiry into the Nature of Practical Theology*. In Lewis S Mudge & James N Poling, (eds). "The Promise of Practical Theology: Formation and Reflection". (Philadelphia: Fortress Press, 1987), 11.

41 Farley, *Interpreting*, 17

42 Thomas W Ogletree, Thomas W. *Dimensions of Practical Theology: Meaning, Action, Self*. In Browning, Don S ed. *Practical Theology* (San Francisco: Harper & Row, 1983), 85.

"What is God calling us to do?" In that context he recalls a familiar saying that he attributes to Bonhoeffer: "You may not chant the psalms unless you stand up for the Jews"[43]. More than that, Bosch points out that most of the New Testament was "written within a missionary context"; in other words, "mission became 'the mother of theology'[44]", and that missionary context, Bosch argues, involves a series of action words – "serving, healing, and reconciling a divided, wounded humanity"[45]. Perhaps we are only now re-discovering that point.

Furthermore, there is a strong contextual element to practical theology; Bevans goes so far as to say that there is no such thing as 'theology'; "there is only *contextual* theology"[46]. By that he means that all theology rises within a particular context, whether that is environmental concern or any one of many other options. He refers to human experience and Christian tradition as the twin poles of theology, and asserts that various cultures have their own preferred ways of doing theology. Whether or not *all* theology is contextual, it is certainly a significant element of practical theology. It follows therefore that the primary reference point for theology is the unfolding of world events rather than the context of the church or the university; or as Ogletree expressed it, "practical theology concerns the concrete enactment of Christian faith in the ongoing course of worldly events"[47]. Thus, context and locus emerge as two related and foundational components of a practical theology methodology, and that may be illustrated in terms of practical eco-mission.

My initial aim was to discover the extent of eco-mission in Australia, and why it is not a stronger part of the Church's agenda. What are the obstacles, and how might they be removed? The rationale behind this was essentially a twofold conviction. First, it seems increasingly evident that planet Earth is in trouble, with climate change, extreme weather, global warming, species loss, and much more. Our survival demands that something be done. Second, the biblical and theological underpinning of our life in the world, in God's world,

---

43 Forrester, Duncan B. *Truthful Action: Explorations in Practical Theology.* (Edinburgh: T & T Clark, 2000), 53
44 Bosch, *Transforming*, 489
45 Bosch, *Transforming*, 494
46 Stephen B Bevans, *Models of Contextual Theology: Faith and Cultures.* (Maryknoll: Orbis Books, 1992), 3
47 Ogletree, *Dimensions*, 94

demands that members of the Christian Church have a responsibility to act. In the case of many churches, however, that is just not happening.

I believe that the resolution of these issues leads irrevocably to the development of a series of models for ecological mission, not only for the Christian Church in Australia, but also for local churches in a variety of particular situations, whether they are urban, rural, inner city, or something else. But given my previous observation that the locus for theology is the world, it should be clear that the change in behaviour patterns I am seeking is not for the sake of the Church, but indeed for the world. That has local and immediate implications in that there are few local situations that are devoid of global implications; or as Bosch puts it, "missiology means globalisation", and that "in order to achieve globalisation, it needs specificity, concretisation"[48].

At one level a concern for environmental care is clearly set within the broad parameters of a global concern, or what could be termed the pain of creation. That of course easily translates into pain not only for masses of people, but also for all living things. At the same time it is important that this global aspect is focussed and concretised in the life of particular areas and ultimately in local Christian communities. Yet out of necessity the "Christian community" in this case is generic rather than specific; this book can do no more than provide general guidelines which will need to be applied in a whole range of different circumstances. A single uniform approach will not work. The guidelines I will offer, which are based on a theology of ecology and Christian mission, will need to be reworked contextually before they can be applied in a particular congregational or regional setting. Thus, it is at the local level that the task of practical theology will continue. The clear purpose of this theological exercise is to generate change, and it therefore fits naturally into a practical theology approach.

Theory and Praxis

We need to say a word about the relationship between theory and praxis; the term *praxis* emphasises not merely an action in itself, but rather more the significance or meaning of the action, or the reflective interaction of theory and practice which can become a means of transformation and change. An earlier belief was that the relationship between theory and praxis was

---

48 Bosch, *Transforming*, 496

essentially linear in character. Traditionally this began with theory, which was always primary and determined any subsequent action, although there are those who would begin at the other end of the spectrum.

But the real situation is another matter, and indeed any theological exercise becomes a complex interaction between theory and praxis. In diagrammatic terms, it becomes an interactive loop, in which theory and praxis "inform and influence each other"[49]. Each new situation forces the individual to interpret the Scripture in a fresh way, to make any necessary personal changes, and in the light of that to interpret the Scripture again as part of an on-going process. It therefore has a forward-moving circular motion, or what Forrester refers to as "the hermeneutic spiral"[50], in which the theologian is constantly moving between the two poles. There can be no doubt that in ecological or environmental terms such a two-way process will be an important part of a practical theology methodology.

At what point though does one enter this hermeneutic spiral? Practical theologians generally assert that the beginning point is invariably the situation, not the theory, although in looking back over perhaps 50 years, and in a great variety of different experiences, my own reflection would suggest that after a period of time the theory-praxis spiral becomes very complex indeed, and it is almost impossible to determine a point of entry for a particular concern. Thus it is a moot point whether my engagement with the specific issue of the environment had its genesis in faith or a commitment to action. Perhaps it was both! From my perspective, the key is that out of practical experience comes engagement in the interaction between theory and praxis that is at the heart of a practical theological method.

A Correlational Approach

One further aspect of this consideration of earth mission relates to what has been called a correlational approach. In other words, having begun with a theological method, we face the question of an inter-disciplinary approach and find that other perspectives are also essential. Thus Browning is able to say that Tracy's view of theology correlates the confessional beginning point of theology with questions shaped both by faith and by other aspects

---

49 Ray S Anderson, *The Shape of Practical Theology: Empowering Ministry with Theological Praxis.* (Downers Grove, Illinois: InterVarsity Press, 2001), 21
50 Forrester, *Truthful,* 28

of our cultural experience"[51]. Tracy's approach to practical theology and the interaction between faith and other cultural experience also serves to describe his approach to theological reflection. He defines it as "the mutually critical correlation of the interpreted theory and praxis of the Christian faith with the interpreted theory and praxis of the contemporary situation"[52]. When considered in the context of the global environment or of eco-theology, I would contend that such a reflective and interpretative inter-disciplinary approach is very helpful, even essential for the outworking of a realistic praxis model.

I have suggested, along with Nash, Moltmann and others, that what has been called the eco-crisis is complex and involves our whole way of life. Thus, the increasingly obvious need for care for our planet Earth is interwoven with a range of issues relating to the human community, providing a rich agenda for eco-theology. Moreover, this is a theology that must be carried out in a very public place, for it raises the question of how it is interacting with other disciplines such as social policy, politics, economics, and science. Each of those areas is important in its own right; however, since ecologists, climatologists and other scientists have clearly added considerably to our understanding of what is happening in our world, and therefore to our awareness of the scope of the crisis, in my view the interface between faith and science becomes an important background dimension of Christian ecological mission.

Partnership of Science and Religion

There has been a perception that science and religion are in opposition to each other, and certainly the relationship between faith and science has never been straightforward. My contention is that there is no real conflict, and that when the nature of both disciplines is properly understood it will be perceived that any lingering difficulties between them persist largely at the fundamentalist fringe of science and faith respectively. The bitter debate was never between science and religion, but between parodies of those disciplines.

Of the various areas in which science and theology may enjoy a fruitful dialogue, one of the most significant is surely the global ecological crisis.

---

51 Don S Browning, *A Fundamental Practical Theology: Descriptive and Strategic Proposals.* (Minneapolis: Fortress Press, 1996), 46

52 D. Tracy, *The Foundations of Practical Theology.* In Browning, Don S ed. 1983. *Practical Theology* (San Francisco: Harper & Row, 1983), 76

This possibility is reflected in the words of the botanist Sir Ghillean Prance. Writing out of a deep faith, Prance stated, "It is no longer enough for me merely to classify and describe the plant species of the Amazon forest; I must also use my research data to address issues of deforestation, pollution, starvation and other problems that surround us today. I am a much more concerned person because my faith helps to remove more selfish motives"[53].

For some decades now, as I have noted, ecologists have been monitoring a whole range of scientific data, and have been issuing dire warnings to any who would listen; sadly, until relatively recently that was a minority. In recent decades an increasing volume of ecological theology has taken the scientific data seriously, and then proceeded to build or rediscover a true biblical theology within that context. It is a prime example of how science and religion may interact effectively, to foster increased awareness of and concern not only about climate change, but many other ecological issues as well, and thus it is a genuine practical theology carried forward in the public arena.

Towards Consonance

Any approach that seeks to keep science and theology apart is doomed, and the two disciplines must at least be in a constructive dialogue with each other. But there is one further step, and it is suggested in Polkinghorne's term "consonance"[54]; it is this, I believe, that offers the best possibility for interaction. In this model, each maintains its autonomy in its acknowledged domain, but "the statements they make must be capable of appropriate reconciliation with each other in overlap regions"; in other words, "the answers to 'How?' and to 'Why?' questions must fit together without strain"[55]. If Humphreys is right, and there is only one "building of truth", then such an approach is essential.

In his analysis of the development of a theological doctrine of creation, Moltmann identifies three distinct phases of understanding. The first stage is that the biblical narrative and pre-scientific images of the universe were

53 Ghillean Prance, *A Talent for Science*. In Berry, R.J. ed. *Real Science, Real Faith*. (Eastbourne, Sussex: Monarch, 1991), p.63

54 John Polkinghorne, *Science and Theology: an Introduction*. (London: SPCK; Minneapolis: Fortress Press, 1998), 118

55 Polkinghorne, *Science*, 22

fused into "a religious cosmology"[56]. Second, when science freed itself from this early view of cosmology, faith tended to retreat to a personal belief in creation. Now, Moltmann suggests, "theology and science have entered a third stage in their relationship"[57]. There are several major factors driving this new symbiotic relationship.

The first factor is nothing less than the maturing of both theological and scientific thought, and a realisation that some previously held positions were simply wrong. Such disciplines are never static, but are by definition fluid and evolving in their quest for truth. Moltmann identifies a second and related factor that adds weight and urgency to the first. Science and theology, he says, "have become companions in tribulation under the pressure of the ecological crisis and the search for the new direction which both must work for, if human beings and nature are to survive at all on this earth"[58].

Moltmann therefore perceives science and theology as being in a new phase of partnership, which, in part, he expresses in these terms: "The sciences have shown us how to understand creation as nature. Now theology must show how nature is to be understood as God's creation"[59].

Emotive responses

It is almost inevitable, and perhaps even necessary, that responses to this crisis can at times have an emotive edge; two examples may be cited. In a draft paper for a conference on critical issues, Gerald Barney discusses many of the issues that have been canvassed above. In it he states, "I think we have reached a fork in the road to the future. Over the lifetime of our children, we humans will either achieve the one possible solution – a just, sustainable development for the whole earth – or we will lose everything." He goes on to ask the leaders of all faith communities, "What Shall We Do?"[60]. Certainly it is not only the theologians who should heed the warning, for quite clearly the situation is becoming steadily more serious than it was in 1990.

---

56 Moltmann, *God in Creation*, 33
57 Moltmann, *God in Creation*, 34
58 Moltmann, *God in Creation*, 34
59 Moltmann, *God in Creation*, 38
60 G.O. Barney, *What Shall we Do?* (Arlington, VA: Institute for 21st Century Studies), 1990), p.35.

The "emotive edge" is even starker in Fox's impassioned plea: "Mother Earth is dying. Are we … our mother's keeper? Is Mother Earth herself not the ultimate *anawim*, the most neglected of the suffering, voiceless ones today? And along with her, the soil, forests, species, birds, and waters are not being heard where legislators gather, where judges preside, and where believers gather to worship. Is the human race involved in a matricide that is also ecocide, geocide, suicide, and even deicide?"[61]. However, as I will argue, an emotive response will only be of value if it leads to actual changes in environmental behaviour.

Conclusion

In this chapter I have sought to identify the main parameters of what may be called the eco-crisis, and have identified two broad areas of concern. In the first instance the considerable volume of concerning scientific data about global ecology represents not only a note of warning, but also a profound sense of urgency. The impact of climate change alone on all forms of life is most significant, but when taken together with the impact of a range of social justice and compassion issues on the lives of people and communities, it reaches a new and more complex level.

There is one last word, however, that may be both provocative and helpful. Ian Lowe cites Peter Ellyard, who pointed out that the Chinese word for "crisis" consists of two characters representing "danger" and "opportunity". Thus, Lowe's assessment is that "the situation is serious and demands our attention, but it is not hopeless"[62]. I have argued that the issues are wide ranging and certainly not limited to ecology. But the challenge is clear – to see the danger signals, and to rise to meet the opportunity they afford.

In this chapter I have considered some of the foundational principles on which this study of Christian earth mission is based. This began with a study of the formative issues of hermeneutics, which is essential for understanding and interpreting data. The notion of a hermeneutic of suspicion was shown to be especially relevant in terms of enabling an ecological reading of the Scriptures.

---

61 M. Fox. *The Coming of the Cosmic Christ,* (North Blackburn, Vic.: Collins Dove), 1988), p.17.

62 Ian Lowe, *Living in the Hothouse: how global warming affects Australia.* (Melbourne: Scribe Publications, 2005), p.8.

I have described a practical theology paradigm as an approach to theology that covers the whole of human existence. In this regard I have also shown the relevance of context and locus, as well as the inter-active relationship of theory and praxis in a "hermeneutic spiral". In sum, while practical theology will inevitably include some largely in-Church elements related to ministry, it must above all be focussed on the larger arena of God's concern – the world itself. It must move beyond the pervasive dualism that shuns matter or the world as evil or irrelevant to spirituality, and grasp that it is the world God loves, and the Church is in the world for the sake of the world.

I have also considered the relationship between faith and science, and concluded that far from being in conflict, the disciplines of science and theology may operate in cooperation to provide a better understanding of the environment and its care. In sum, this work and the methods employed will involve a constant dialogue between the twin poles of theory and praxis in seeking an adequate response to God's perceived purpose in the world.

CHAPTER THREE

Approaches to Environmental Issues

In these days in which there is a large and increasing range of ways in which viewpoints may be expressed and in which the environment can become an ideological plaything, many of us glean our information from sources that are not necessarily reliable. But people have long responded in a variety of ways to the natural environment. The purpose of this chapter is to discuss a number of those responses, beginning with some that easily become utilitarian and exploitative, and which therefore offer little or no assistance in enabling positive ecological outcomes. Such approaches are relatively common in the community at large and even within the Christian community, so it is important that they be identified. We will then move on to responses that are life or God centred and which offer greater hope for the future.

Nature Disenchanted

The first approach may be described as the disenchantment of nature, and this is set against the background of White's famous 1967 assertion[1] that the Christian doctrine of dominion is largely to blame for the current crisis. I have argued against White's position elsewhere, and we do not need to re-visit that issue at length here. But in asserting the need for an environmental ethic, Strong and Rosenfield[2] refer to two ethical systems which they believe have contributed to our current difficulties. One of those relates to the Judeo-Christian ethic, and here they summarise the response of some of White's critics. For example, they refer to Wright, a biologist who argues that while Christianity nurtured science and technology in the early stages, it was nevertheless the scientists themselves, and not Christianity, who are responsible for the destruction that resulted from their activities. Similarly they note the view of Yi-Fu Tuan, a geographer, that similar destruction

---

1 Lynn White Jnr. *The Historical Roots of our Ecological Crisis.* Washington DC: "Science" (The American Association for the Advancement of Science), Vol 155, Number 3767, 10th March 1967.

2 DH Strong and Rosenfield. *Ethics or Expediency: an Environmental Question.* In KS Shrader-Frechette, "Environmental Ethics". (Pacific Grove, CA: Boxwood Press, 1991).

also took place in a non-Christian traditional China. My contention is that exploitation was by no means limited to the "Christian" West, and that Christian practice has varied widely. Nevertheless, the conclusion reached by Strong and Rosenfield is that "enlightened self-interest can form the basis for an effective, generally acceptable environmental ethic"[3]. I am arguing that such an approach on its own is not enough, and that an enlightened Christian faith has a large part to play in the development of an environmental ethic.

White is undoubtedly correct in his contention that human self-centredness is at the root of the eco crisis; his assertion that Christianity is the most human-centred religion the world has seen is another matter, and, I suggest, is at best highly doubtful. In any event, the real issue relates to the origin of ecological exploitation. It is here that McGrath[4] makes an important contribution to the debate by tracing the history of this exploitation from its genesis in ancient Greece, where the dream of domination was expressed in Plato's dialogues in which Protagoras says "man is the measure of all things"[5]. McGrath goes on to indicate that the Greek idea was reversed to some extent in the Middle Ages with the Christian belief that there was some intrinsic ordering of nature, that it was something that was to be respected. Humanity was seen as part of a greater cosmic ordering, perhaps even at the apex, but with no right to alter the course or change the contours of nature.

But two points need to be noted. First, the history of Christian thought in this regard is ambiguous. The second point, which may seem to complicate the issue, is that there can be no neat division between scientists and Christians; indeed it is true that prior to the 19th century most Westerners, including scientists, embraced some form of Christian faith.

Not surprisingly, the ancient classic ideas were again to the fore in the Renaissance period. But with McGrath, I contend that the root of the problem is the secular creed of 20th century Western culture rising out of the 18th century Enlightenment. This included a rejection of authority, including that of God, and invoked the supremacy of human reason. For

---

3 Strong and Rosenfield, *Ethics,* 13
4 Alister McGrath, *The Re-enchantment of nature: Science, Religion, and the Human Sense of Wonder.* (London: Hodder & Stoughton, 2002
5 cited in McGrath, *Re-enchantment,* 55

some, religion was harmless; for others it was debasing, oppressive, and required forced elimination. There was a sense of freedom; the shackles were off. The implications of such an approach were expressed with stark clarity by Winwood Reade in his influential 1872 book, *The Martyrdom of Man*. Reade expressed the idea that "nature must be disenchanted, evacuated of any concept of spiritual or religious significance, before it can be harnessed to human progress and the advancement of civilization". His words describe what was perceived to be "the triumph of human genius over the crudities of nature"[6].

But contrary to McGrath, Vogel is actually reflecting the views of Horkheimer and Adorno rather than his own with the assertion that the roots of ecological exploitation are to be found in the promotion of reason at the expense of religion; Vogel states, "The project of the Enlightenment aims above all at the domination *of nature*. Disenchanted and objectified nature, appearing now in the guise of meaningless matter, is seen by the Enlightenment simply as something to be overcome and mastered for human purposes, and not to be imitated, propitiated, or religiously celebrated"[7]. Behind that development is the idea that humanity is of central and defining importance. Vogel's own view is a little more complex, but his essential conclusion may be expressed thus: "The responsibility we have for the world we inhabit is a *practical* responsibility; we produce that world through our practices and can change it only by changing those practices"[8]. Put another way, as McGrath suggests, when an anthropocentric worldview is "provided with the tools that enable it to achieve its goal of dominating nature … the environment is really in trouble"[9].

This approach continued into the Victorian period, when social and technological advances rose out of that sustained human quest and went hand in hand with the advance of science. I have acknowledged the culpability of some theology, but I am arguing that the real problem lies in the fact that technology, and to a large extent modern industrialised nations, are still bound by the approach that originated in ancient Greece and which was dramatically renewed in the period of the Enlightenment.

---

6 McGrath, *Re-enchantment*, 57
7 Steven Vogel, *Against Nature: the Concept of Nature in Critical Theory*. (Albany, New York: State University of New York Press, 1996), 52
8 Vogel, *Against Nature*, 172
9 McGrath, *Re-enchantment*, 54

Sadly, we have become all too familiar with the destructive results and environmental degradation of unbridled development.

The Econocentric Approach

The heirs of such an approach are still clearly in evidence in the modern era. What I call econocentrism, for example, pins everything on short-term economic and political gain, as in the famous line of a Clinton Advisor, "it's the economy stupid", and while not readily recognised in the literature, is common enough. It should also be said that some of the opposition to any form of environmental concern is uninformed, and one would have to say somewhat hysterical and cynical, and does not rate serious consideration.

At a more serious level it may be argued that cultural, technological, and social forces are factors that have fostered exploitation. In that regard, a second system to which Strong and Rosenfield[10] refer is expediency, that whatever provides the greatest benefit to the largest number of people at the lowest cost must necessarily be good; this relates to the notion that the modern ecological crisis, at least in part, results from the pursuit of short-term economic self-interest. Such an approach may be witnessed regularly as governments and big business make decisions on that basis. It is arguable that the situation is changing, but historically there has often been a lack of capacity or political will to translate that vision into eco-friendly policies that will begin to make a difference.

Notions of growth and progress need to be carefully scrutinised. In popular economics expressed in political and business circles, the notion of a continually growing economy is taken as both possible and essential. But from the perspective of Earth as a planet with finite resources, such an attitude makes little sense. The widespread perception that human-kind must continually progress or we will go backwards begs the question as to how "progress" is to be defined.

There are some things that money cannot buy. As Gowdy and O'Hara state, "The economy-environment conflict ultimately arises from the impossibility of economic markets to place ecologically meaningful values on the functions and attributes of the biophysical world"11. Since natural resources appear to

---

10 Strong and Rosenfield, *Ethics.*
11 John Gowdy and Sabine O'Hara. *Economic Theory for Environmentalists.* (Delray Beach, Florida: St Lucie Press, 1995), 11.

be free except for the cost of development, the risk of exploitation is always real. We tend to undervalue the things that come cheaply!

René Doubos expressed the view that "the solution to the environmental crisis will not be found in a retreat from the Judeo-Christian tradition or from technological civilization", but will be found in "a new definition of progress, based on a better knowledge of nature and on a willingness to change our ways accordingly"[12]. In a similar vein, Granberg-Michaelson refers to an address by Herman Daly, an economist, to the Rio Earth Summit in 1992, in which he spoke of our failure to recognize that any economy is only a subsystem of the "larger, finite, non-growing and closed ecosystem on which it is fully dependent"; a consequence of that failure has been the human inclination to enrich the present at the expense of the future and of other species, an approach which he described as "sinful"[13].

It should be noted that the natural association of economy solely with financial systems which is common-place today in fact did not develop until the 19th or 20th century; further, such a narrowness of definition clearly leads to distortion. The etymology of the word "economy" suggests another approach. It originated in ancient Greece, and combines two words – "eco" is derived from *oikos* which means "house", and "nomy" derives from *nomos*, a law or principle. Thus, as the Word Power website explains[14], "the word 'economy' literally means 'the principles to maintain our house'. Now whether that 'house' is government, Earth, or family is relative." Such an understanding of economy is far more holistic in its approach than popular usage focussed solely on financial considerations would suggest.

At the same time, it must be acknowledged that there are some occasional signs of hope, as business people band together to seek ecologically sustainable and economically viable outcomes. One example of that is the Australian Business Council for Sustainable Energy. In recent times there have also been moves to spend the necessary funds to try to generate clean coal technology, although efforts to access the economic and environmental benefits of renewable energy would be more productive in the long term. But an econocentric approach that ignores ecological sustainability is

12 René Dubos, *Franciscan Conservation versus Benedictine Stewardship*. In Berry, R.J. ed., "Environmental Stewardship". (London and New York: T & T Clark International, 2006), 58
13 Granberg-Michaelson, *Redeeming*, 5
14 www.babeled.com

nonsense, and must be rejected. Perhaps a more significant danger is that of businesses operating in an essentially non-sustainable way, but making minimal environmental concessions in order to project a "green" image. The use of the prefix "eco" does not of itself make a product climate friendly! The emphasis here is on "image" rather than on reality, in which case it represents deception. The Stern Review in 2006 is primarily about the economics of climate change, and its conclusion is clear: "The evidence shows that ignoring climate change will eventually damage economic growth"; or in other words, "the benefits of strong, early action considerably outweigh the costs"[15]. There are two issues in that. First, action to protect the environment will inevitably be costly in the short to medium term, but the failure to take action will result in even more serious economic consequences in the future. Second, evidence is starting to emerge that in some cases a genuinely environmentally friendly approach to industry may have some short term benefits as well. Indeed it is true that the economy is a wholly-owned subsidiary of the environment.

Anthropocentrism

An anthropocentric or human-centred approach is common, and Thomas Berry[16] is not alone in having a problem with it, certainly in the context of the environment; he regards the move to a life-centred biocentrism as essential and basic. But anthropocentrism comes at three levels, and as the name suggests, it is an approach that places humankind at the centre of experienced reality. Further, it is an integral part of any ecologically exploitative system. Yet it is also important to note as an issue in its own right. In its worst form it leads to damaging domination and devastation of the earth; at its best it provides an enlightened and caring stewardship, although in reality that insight comes from elsewhere. The concern here will be with the former, and we need to explore a number of issues concerning anthropocentrism and the relationship of humans to the rest of creation.

The primary issue here is a theological belief that a biblically based Christian faith is not only concerned solely with human salvation, but also that nature is there for humankind's benefit. This could almost be styled as anti-nature. Some examples of mainly historical interest may be considered

---

15 Stern, *Review,* ii
16 Thomas Berry, *The Dream of the Earth.* (San Francisco: Sierra Club Books, 1998).

briefly. Opinions differ concerning Calvin's position and the environmental impact of his commentaries. According to Bradley, Calvin could say that the end of all things is for the benefit of man[17], suggesting that humans have a God-given right to deal with nature more or less as they wish. At the same time, while it is true that Calvin tended to an anthropocentric view, and his work is a product of its time, there is also an element of moderation and care. In reference to Genesis 2:15, for example, Calvin states, "Let him who possesses a field, so partake of its yearly fruits, that he may not suffer the ground to be injured by his negligence; but let him endeavour to hand it down to posterity as he received it, or even better cultivated"[18]. But as Northcott argues, his focus on care was counter-balanced by a notion of the depravity of nature, the rise of an instrumentalist view that did not regard the purposes of God, and also the anthropocentric emphasis of some later reformers. Thus, it may be argued, perhaps a little unfairly, that Calvin's approach played a part in the encouragement of the increased domination of nature and the discarding of ethical limitations on its use, whether or not that was his intention.

An observation attributed to Professor Dickie in 1930, and cited by Northcott, is more clear-cut: "The world exists for our sakes and not for its own"[19]. His reason is essentially that only personal beings can respond to Love, and therefore the world is only a means, and not an end. Perhaps even more shocking is a statement concerning animals attributed to John Henry Newman: "We may use them, we may destroy them at our pleasure ... for our own ends, for our own benefit or satisfaction"[20]. If that is a fair reflection of Newman's position, it is anthropocentric through and through. At the same time, the good faith of people like Newman should not be doubted. The key issue here, as I will argue, is that the biblical message has been widely misunderstood throughout Christian history.

Derrick speaks of "the feeling of alienation, the sense of a sharp and sad discontinuity between mankind and the rest of nature"[21]; and that, he

---

17 Ian Bradley, *God is Green: Ecology for Christians*. (New York, NY: Doubleday, 1992), 12.

18 John Calvin, Reprint edition, translated J King. *Commentary on the First Book of Moses called Genesis*. (Grand Rapids, Mich.: W.B. Eerdmans Publishing, 1948), 125

19 Michael S Northcott, *The Environment and Christian Ethics*. (Cambridge: Cambridge University Press, 1996), 13

20 Bradley, *God is Green*, 13

21 C. Derrick, *The Delicate Creation*. (Old Greenwich, Conn.: Devin-Adair Co.,1972), 54

says, is based on Gnostic and Manichaean systems of thought. In fact the dualism base is wider than that, and it is clear that some theologies still carry undertones of a Gnostic or Neo-Platonic dualism. Derrick goes on to argue that these persistent tendencies "wear secular garments", although churches "have not been immune from their infection"[22]. One outcome of that has been the tendency of humans to regard themselves as separate from and superior to other living beings and the rest of creation. They have taken to heart an anthropocentric version of Genesis 1:28 and the forecast of Genesis 9:2, that "the fear and dread of you" shall rest on all living creatures. I am arguing, however, that "dominion" does not give a licence to despoil and pillage the earth, and that the text in context would lead away from that possibility.

There is a second form of anthropocentrism that is not directly detrimental to the environment, but I contend that it is not helpful either. Here Christian theology is seen as having no ecological agenda, either positive or negative, but the focus is on human salvation exclusively. Vogtle, Eduard Schweizer, Bultmann, Karl Barth, and many others essentially belong in this category. The question is whether the Greek New Testament words *panta, kosmos,* and *ktisis* refer only to people, or whether, as Markus Barth[23] suggests, that more frequently they include all created things. Reumann[24] makes it clear that he is only interested in the human aspect of creation. In any event, given the broader sweep of the biblical literature and a vastly different context today, it is probably somewhat irrelevant whether Paul had only humans in mind, or the wider creation. Kaufman[25] is a further example of the same school of thought. His claim is that because humans are ontologically different from the natural world, they are therefore above the rest of the natural world; the outcome of such a position is a somewhat objectified view of nature, which is then more vulnerable to exploitation.

There is a third approach – the recognition of a significant ecological agenda, but from an anthropocentric point of view. A prime example of this school of thought is Thomas Derr, who has long argued for a human focus,

---

22 Derrick, *Delicate*, 67

23 Markus Barth, *Christ and all Things*. In Hooker, MD and Wilson SG eds. *Paul and Paulinism*. (London: SPCK., 1982

24 J. Reumann, *Creation and New Creation.* (Minneapolis: Augsburg Press, 1982

25 Kaufman 1972

but one that is devoid of human mastery. In his 1996 work in company with Nash and Neuhaus, Derr reiterates a view that he first propounded 25 years earlier; he states, "Actually I do not mind being called an anthropocentrist, though I would rather say simply (Christian) 'humanist', meaning that my priority in matters ecological is humankind"[26]. As I will show later, in the final analysis the wellbeing of humankind cannot be separated from what has been termed the web of life. However, Derr's argument is that this should lead to a theology of responsible stewardship of the earth. In this view, nature is seen as a complement to the primary drama of redemption that takes place in history. Such an approach is a step in the right direction, but one may well wonder if an ecologically aware anthropocentrism is not close to a contradiction in terms.

Biocentrism

In general terms, biocentrism is at the opposite extreme from anthropocentrism, and holds that all life has inherent value and is indissolubly connected. However, proponents of this view approach it with some differing perspectives and emphases which render the task of definition somewhat difficult. As a starting point, however, Birch's attempt may be considered adequate for our present purposes. He proposes a Christian biocentric ethic as one that encompasses the whole of life, that "the recognition of intrinsic value in creatures besides ourselves makes an ethical claim upon us to recognise our obligation toward them"[27]. In an earlier work, Birch extended the definition of "neighbour" to include all participants in life. For him, "the central principle of a biocentric ethic is that we deal with living organisms appropriately when we rightly balance their intrinsic value with their instrumental value"[28]. It should be noted, however, that many non-Christian proponents of biocentrism would share a similar ethic.

One of the fundamental tenets of all biocentrism is the notion that not only is all life significant, but also that there is an essential unity binding all life. That emerges clearly in a scientific approach, through which we

26 Thomas S Derr, *Environmental Ethics and Christian Humanism*. (Nashville, TN: Abingdon Press, 1996), 18
27 Charles Birch, *Regaining Compassion for Humanity and Nature*. (Kensington NSW: New South Wales University Press, 1993), 89
28 Birch, *Regaining*, 90

face, in Moltmann's terms, the ultimate choice of "one world or none"[29]. Thus, science has something to say about relationships. As Hart[30] indicates, quantum physics, biology, and chemistry all suggest an intricate pattern of relationships among the entities they study. Similarly, through DNA sampling in recent years, scientific evidence points in the same direction; further, psychologists, sociologists, and anthropologists all indicate a similar outlook. As a result of these realities, Hart concludes that "people might rightly wonder about the appropriateness of regarding the universe as subordinate to human interests"[31]. Bradley agrees, and argues that quantum physics point to a universe that at its deepest level is "a single unified whole, indivisible and bound together by a simple yet powerful force"[32]. Such a biocentric outlook may also be traced through traditional Aboriginal spirituality, Process Philosophy, Ecofeminism, and Deep Ecology.

An Australian Aboriginal Understanding

The indigenous people of Australia have a particular worldview that is highly relevant in terms of the modern environmental crisis, and it is therefore important to begin to understand their perspective. At the outset it may be said that the whole of traditional Aboriginal life is spiritual in orientation; the dichotomy of sacred and secular finds no meaning for them, since all life is sacred.

This reveals one of the areas of fundamental difference between a traditional Western approach and a traditional Aboriginal spirituality. The potential for a cultural clash is implicit in Hume's observation that "the sacredness of land to Aboriginal people is of paramount importance to traditional spirituality and is of increasing political importance in a country like Australia which bases many of its economic assets on mining and other land exploitative industries"[33].

Notions of the dreaming, totemic systems and an understanding of the land as sacred are all involved. Thus as Hume points out, relationships are

---

29 Moltmann, *God in Creation*, 34
30 John Hart, *What are They Saying about Environmental Theology?* (Mahwah, New Jersey: Paulist Press, 2004).
31 Hart, *What are they saying*, 125
32 Bradley, *God*, 19
33 Lynne Hume, *The Rainbow Serpent, The Cross, and the Fax Machine: Australian Aboriginal Responses to the Bible*. In Mark G Brett, ed. *Ethnicity and the Bible*. (Leiden: E.J. Brill, 1996), 372

of prime importance, involving people with other people, the land, and totems. The inter-connectedness that is the essence of traditional Aboriginal identity is clearly biocentric in character.

"The Dreaming" is one of the central concepts of Aboriginal spirituality, and relates to a time when ancestral heroes roamed the Earth; and since those heroes did not simply create the landscape and move on, but rather became a living part of it in the present, the natural world takes on a new and sacred meaning. The Dreaming collapses past, present, and future into one reality. What that means for Aboriginal people is that the land is much more a spiritual landscape than an economic commodity, and is related to the ancestors who originated in the Dreaming.

The Dreaming therefore becomes the basis on which an Aborigine like Kneebone can see himself as part of the natural environment. In an interview with Catherine Hammond, he expressed his belief that after death, "the spirit will return to the Dreamtime from where it came, it will carry our memories to the Dreamtime and eventually it will return again through birth, either as a human or animal or even trees and rocks"[34]. It is possible that not all Aborigines would fully embrace this view; but equally, that sense of oneness with the natural order, and the sacredness of it, is a very common theme.

The sense of bonding with the land is further emphasised in the totemic belief of the people. In the traditional culture, an Aboriginal child is given a totem of birth, but will eventually belong to several totemic groups. It is not necessary to examine totemism in any detail here; suffice it to say that totem in Aboriginal Australia always has a mystical dimension and is suffused with symbolism. Totemism and Dreaming are part of the one reality for Aboriginal people. Stanner illustrates this very clearly in citing a typical situation of a father taking his young son to a particular special place, where he would say to him, "your Dreaming is there; you want to look after this place ... it is from the first (totemist) man"[35]. He suggests the struggle to find words which may describe this mystical reality, stressing again that "Dreamings (totem entities) come from there; your spirit is

---

34 Catherine Hammond, ed., *Creation Spirituality in the Dreamtime.* (Newtown, NSW: Millennium Books, 1991), 89
35 Stanner 1979, p.135

there"; in other words, there is an unbroken connection "between man, totem, and spirit home"[36].

The implications of such a belief system are clear. The Dreaming and all that it represents becomes the basis for an approach to the land as sacred; it provides a sense of connection between people and the land which means that land must be cared for. As George Rosendale suggests, "When we talk about land, we say, this is our land. Actually it is not our land, we are *caretakers* of this land. Each family within that tribe has certain responsibilities in caring for the land"[37]. He goes on to associate that principle with Genesis 2:15, the divine call to tend the Earth and keep it.

Kneebone and others insist that non-Aborigines also have their Dreaming, their own sense of spiritual identity, and most Australians would have great difficulty in following the Aboriginal belief path very far. However, in the econocentric atmosphere that tends to prevail in these days, we might seek to learn something from Aboriginal biocentric spirituality about our care of the natural environment and our relationship with other life.

Process Philosophy

Process Philosophy began with Alfred North Whitehead, who was an avowed non-Christian, but who is significant in this context for the manner in which he influenced Christian theologians such as Hartshorne and Cobb. Whitehead himself states at the outset that his work is "speculative"[38]; beyond that it is certainly complex and technical in nature, but several basic points may be noted. Whitehead saw everything that comprised the "stuff of reality" as interactive and social; he stated that "each task of creation is a social effort, employing the whole universe"[39]. For him, everything in the universe is in a process of change, each moving towards its own goal; as he states, "self-realization is the ultimate fact of facts"[40]. He pictures the world as an incredible multiplicity of entities in a fluid state, creating and recreating. God is the ultimate point of that process, but God's prime function for Whitehead is in being the element in everything that preserves

---

36 Stanner 1979, p.135

37 Rosendale In Mark G Brett, ed. *Ethnicity and the Bible.* (Leiden: E.J. Brill, 1996), 372

38 Alfred North Whitehead, *Process and Reality: an Essay in Cosmology.* Corrected edition, David R Griffin and Donald W Sherburne, eds. (New York and London: The Free Press, 1978). 3

39 Whitehead, *Process*, 223

40 Whitehead, *Process*, 222

its uniqueness and speeds it towards its combination and unity. The point of connection between Whitehead's philosophy and environmental thinking is, as Collins[41] suggests, in his emphasis on the inter-subjectivity of all reality; Whitehead states, "The physical world is bound together by a general type of relatedness which constitutes it into an extensive continuum"[42]. It follows that in a social universe where nothing exists in isolation, notions such as anthropocentrism and dualism could have little meaning.

Eco-feminism

In a similar way, ecofeminist philosophy may be regarded as biocentric through and through, and in general terms most ecofeminists would agree with the assertion that a hierarchical view of the world, with its assumed superiority and inferiority, is the main cause of the oppression of both women and nature. Ruether's Christian eco-feminism, for example, brings together elements of ecology and feminism "in their full, or deep forms, and explores how male domination of women and domination of nature are interconnected, both in cultural ideology and in social structures"[43]. Elements of eco-justice are also involved.

The term eco-feminism embraces a range of views, not all of which are Christian or even compatible with each other. Some versions of this philosophy not only lead right outside any form of mainstream religion, but also at times beyond any form of religious expression at all. However, ecofeminists would be united in the twin goals of the liberation of women and of nature; even more, as Fowler states, "Ecofeminist literature is suffused with the exaltation of community as a goal"[44]. Thus, eco-feminists generally seek an end of dualisms and hierarchical structures, which can sometimes mean that for them the boundaries between people and nature begin to disappear[45].

---

41 Paul Collins, *God's Earth: Religion as if Matter Really Mattered.* (North Blackburn, Vic: Dove (HarperCollins), 1995
42 Whitehead, *Process*, 96
43 Ruether, *Gaia*, 2
44 Robert B Fowler, *The Greening of Protestant Thought.* (Chapel Hill & London: The University of North Carolina Press, 1995), 127
45 Fowler, *Greening*, 125-6

Deep Ecology

Deep Ecology is usually traced back to a Norwegian philosopher, Arne Naess, who in his famous 1973 essay sought to develop what he regarded as a "deeper, more spiritual approach to Nature"[46] Yet while deep ecology, like other philosophies, does not represent a single unified or coherent approach, several dominant themes emerge. Clearly, for Naess it represents not just a marginal reform of society, but a substantial reorientation of our whole approach to life and its values.

According to Naess, there are two ultimate and closely related norms; the first of these is self-realization. But this goes beyond the traditional Western sense of individualism to a much broader context. Devall and Sessions' claim is that "deep ecology is emerging as a way of developing a new balance and harmony between individuals, communities, and all of Nature"[47]. Thus, our full maturing as persons takes place in the context of organic wholeness, in which we see ourselves alongside "whales, grizzly bears, whole rain forest ecosystems, mountains and rivers, the tiniest microbes in the soil, and so on"[48].

If deep ecology stopped at that point, and left the argument with the affirmation that everything is connected", the situation would change completely; after all, such a position would be shared by Process Philosophy, Eco-feminism, and as I will argue, with a biblical Christian position as well. But deep ecology moves on to what might be regarded as the most definitive feature of this philosophy, namely its belief in the notion of bio-equality. This is the assertion, as Devall and Sessions state, that "all things in the biosphere have an equal right to live and blossom and to reach their own … self-realization within the larger Self-realization"[49]. Thus, humans are just one species in the biotic community, with no greater claim than any other. Perhaps it comes as no great surprise to find what many would consider to be extraordinary claims at the extreme end of the biotic equality spectrum. Naess himself was realist enough to recognise that in practical terms complete biotic equality is unrealistic, since existence would not be possible on those terms. In one form or another, all life feeds on other life.

---

46 Bill Devall and George Sessions. *Deep Ecology*. (Salt Lake City, Utah: Gibbs Smith, 1985), 65.
47 Devall and Sessions, *Deep*, 7
48 Devall and Sessions, *Deep*, 67
49 Devall and Sessions, *Deep*, 67

God and the web of life

The nature of the relationship between humans and the rest of creation is an important issue, and it is clear that in spite of differing emphases, the philosophies or spiritualities I have considered thus far would all agree that humankind is part of what may be called "the web of life", and not above it. I am arguing, however, that there are difficulties with forms of biocentrism in which the fundamental unity of life is allowed to become an equality that virtually eliminates difference. Not only does that distort the relationship within "the web of life", but also it is ecologically unhelpful, unrealistic, and may be difficult to reconcile with Christian theology.

Once that extreme position is set aside, however, as I will show, there is strong theological support for the biocentric argument about the interdependence and unity of life. The notion that life exists in relationship thus becomes an important corrective to the domination theory. Within a wide context of known reality, Moltmann has suggested that "the scientists have shown us how to understand Creation as nature. Now theology must show science how nature is to be understood as God's creation"[50]. It is with that thought that theology has something to contribute to an understanding of life and relationships in the natural world that I turn to theocentrism.

Theocentrism – God and Life

It is clear, I believe, that in spite of the varied approaches, there is nevertheless a common or unifying thread running through the life-centred approaches considered earlier, leading to the conclusion that there are some valuable insights in a biocentric approach. I believe, however, that in its pure form it is inadequate, especially in the context of trying to encourage ecological mission in a Christian context. It is my conviction that a properly understood God-centred or theocentric approach offers the best hope of a balanced understanding of a global ecosystem and our place in it. In other words, with God as Creator at the centre, everything can assume its rightful place; and while it is true that adherents of an anthropocentric position could also agree with that statement, I will be interpreting it in more biocentric terms. From an Orthodox perspective, Gregorios reminds us that the basic distinction in the Patristic literature is not between God and humanity, but

---

50 Moltmann, *God in Creation*, 38

between "He who truly is" and "the things that merely exist"[51]. The essential unity of all life is recognised, with humans as part of creation; but the special role and responsibility of people made in the image of God is also recognised. Even so, there is nothing automatic about it.

It should be noted that a theocentric approach in and of itself is not enough. Probably most of those who focus the Christian message solely on the human condition would also believe that they are "theocentric". But in Bouma-Prediger's phrase[52], what is required is a "creation-encompassing theocentrism"; the distinction is very important. Gnanakan[53] also explicitly advocates this approach. At the risk of introducing a somewhat clumsy term, "theistic biocentrism" may be more precise than theocentrism, and communicate a more accurate picture of God's relationship with the creation.

Diversity in the Theistic Approach

It would be misleading, however, to suggest that theocentrism reflects a single unified position. Paul Santmire[54] has helpfully shown that there are three major schools of thought involved here, although it must be noted that there can be considerable variation even within those three schools. Reconstructionists, he says, begin with the assumption that the Christian faith offers few resources for dealing with the eco-crisis, and therefore believe that a complete overhaul of the classic kerygmatic tradition is necessary. In doing so they may even look to an eclectic range of "new" spiritualities, Eastern religions, and New Age concepts. Matthew Fox, Thomas Berry, Rosemary Radford Ruether, and Sallie McFague are identified as examples of this school. Their radical approach to Christianity is capable of ample illustration, not least in terms of their concept of God. Suffice it to say that while there can be no doubt that reconstructionists are eco-friendly, it is doubtful if their approach would have more than a marginal impact upon the church at large, especially in areas where a conservative approach is dominant.

---

51 Paulos Gregorios. 1978. *The Human Presence: an Orthodox View of Nature.* (Geneva: WCC Publications, 19778), 24
52 Steven Bouma-Prediger, *For the Beauty of the Earth: a Christian Vision for Creation Care.* (Grand Rapids, MI: Baker Academic, 2001),103
53 Ken Gnanakan, *God's World: Biblical Insights for a Theology of the Environment.* (London: SPCK, 1999
54 H Paul Santmire, *Nature Reborn: the Ecological and Cosmic Promise of Christian Theology.* (Minneapolis: Fortress Press, 2000), 1300

At the more conservative end of the spectrum are the apologists who are keen to stress Christianity's green credentials, and consequently the need for good stewardship of the earth. There is therefore a form of eco-friendly anthropocentrism involved here, but as Derr would insist, it is legitimately there. The work of the World Council of Churches for a "just, participatory, and sustainable society" comes in this category. Apologists include Thomas Derr, Douglas John Hall, and others. The question whether the term "stewardship" is adequate to inspire a new generation of eco-awareness must be held over until chapter 5.

Santmire himself identifies with the third option, the revisionist school. "The revisionists work within the milieu of classical Christian thought as defined by the ecumenical creeds"[55], and give high priority to biblical interpretation. Such a theology of nature, Santmire says, will be "biblical, christological, ecological, and ecclesiological"[56], but it will take on the more universal scope of Colossians 1:15-20 and reflected by Sittler. Moltmann is identified as revisionist, as are Sittler, James Nash, Fretheim, Edwards, McDonagh, Hallman, and Rasmussen.

Santmire's categories, while helpful, should not be regarded as absolute, and Ruether is surely correct in stating that Christians can be "lured into ecological consciousness only if they see that it grows in some ways from the soil in which they are planted"[57]. It is for that reason, I believe, that while a viable eco-mission theology can be built on the foundation of any one of these three schools of thought, it is most likely to rise out of either the apologetic or revisionist approach.

Theocentric Views of the Unity of life

As in the case of the biocentric philosophies, theocentric views may also vary in their understanding. Nevertheless, there is a strong biblical tradition that holds the essential unity of all life, with humans recognised as part of creation. Clearly, the biblical references to heaven and earth, sun, moon, plants, trees, birds, fish, animals etc mean that God is concerned with all of these. In writing of the creation event, Westermann states, "The Bible is speaking of a definitive event which concerns not only humankind but

---

55 Santmire, *Nature,* 1301
56 Santmire, *Nature,* 1302
57 Ruether, *Gaia,* 207

the whole of creation"[58]. Humans, however, need both humility in their creaturehood, and also an acceptance of the responsibility of stewardship[59]. As I will indicate below, Ruether develops this view, based on the concept of a covenant relationship.

This, however, raises issues related to the notion of biotic equality. Sallie McFague is one who draws attention to both similarity and difference among living things, and in doing so she differs markedly from deep ecologists and some other eco-feminists. If we go back far enough, she says, we inevitably come to a common ancestry, whether we are an oak tree or a human being. We are inexorably bound together with all other life in intricate and complex relationships. Denis Edwards describes that interconnection in a most thought provoking way in terms of the origin of all life in the stars as he declares "We are all inter-connected in the one story of the universe, and we are all made from stardust"[60]. It should also be noted that God's covenant with Noah specifically included all life, and not just humankind (Gen 9:12).

However, as McFague argues, when "things are so profoundly interrelated and inter-dependent that they are, in effect, one"[61], this denial of both diversity and individuality provides a weak basis for an environmental ethic. However, she says, there is "one crucial difference that separates human beings from all other life forms, and it may be the difference that makes all the difference: we are, to our knowledge, the only creatures on the planet who *know* the common creation story, the only creatures who not only participate in it but *know* that they do"[62]. For McFague, it is the common creation story that provides the paradigm for responding to other life, and indeed for understanding their difference from us. Thus she affirms both unity and difference, and while acknowledging some value in deep ecology, asserts that "what is missing in deep ecology is a developed sense of *difference*"[63]. Birch would agree with that position. He argues, for

---

58 Claus Westermann, 1971. *Creation.* (London: SPCK, 1971), 177.
59 Sean McDonagh, *To Care for the Earth: A Call to a New Theological Passion for the Earth.* (London: Geoffrey Chapman, 1986
60 Denis Edwards, *Ecology at the Heart of Faith* p 12.
61 Sallie McFague, *The Body of God: an Ecological Theology.* (Minneapolis; London: Fortress; SCM, 1993), 127
62 McFague, *The Body,* 60
63 McFague, *Body,* 128

example, that all creatures do not have the same rights or intrinsic value, and that some distinctions are needed if our environmental ethic is not to become "confused and impractical"[64].

I conclude that it is valid to argue for a profound unity or "web of life", and to discern an enormous amount of inter-relationship among living things or beings, but also that it is important to sufficiently acknowledge the importance of difference between human and other life. Without moving to an anthropocentric position, it must be said that from a biblical and theological point of view, God's concern for all life must be balanced by an understanding of the unique human place in the divine economy.

Conclusion

In this chapter I have identified a number of approaches to the global ecological condition that I have identified as exploitative. That certainly is the case with the first three, relating to domination, the disenchantment of nature, and econocentrism, since the approach of each of these works to the detriment of the natural world. Even though there is room for some quite different responses to have potential as a basis for positive ecological action, such exploitative approaches almost by definition disqualify themselves, and they must therefore be rejected. The case of anthropocentrism however is more complex, and while the first form I identified is clearly exploitative and must therefore join the other approaches in rejection, it is equally clear that some forms of anthropocentrism may in fact lend themselves, in part at least, to some kind of ecological action. That must be stated with some caution however, and any anthropocentric philosophy, even one that claims a degree of biblical mandate, should be treated with suspicion.

In a more environmentally positive sense I have outlined a biocentric or life-centred approach in a number of forms, not the least of which is Aboriginal spirituality. But I have also argued the case for a life and God-centred approach, and pointed to the inter-connectedness of all life. We turn next to the Biblical and Theological basis of eco-mission.

---

64 Birch, *Regaining*, 105-6

CHAPTER FOUR

The Biblical and Theological Basis of Eco-Mission

We have considered some of the dimensions of what has loosely been called the eco-crisis, and I have suggested that while those factors are very important, ecological mission essentially builds on a theological base. It is hard to over-emphasise the importance of such an approach. In this chapter therefore we will consider a number of critical issues before going on to outline some of the theological aspects involved.

Critical issues and Questions

How might the Christian relate to the natural world and the eco-crisis as outlined in chapter 2? It could be argued that historically the eco-crisis has been compounded by what may be regarded as a theological crisis. There are some people who would have a problem with the very concept of ecological theology. Santmire, for example, is summarising the findings of his historical survey when he states, "According to a large number of contemporary theological writers … Christian theology never has had, nor should it have, a substantive ecological dimension"[1]. He goes on to describe the theological tradition of the West in terms of ambiguity, and in many ways the debate is located around that point.

Ambiguity and Ancient Roots

Part of the problem may be the way in which theological and political issues can be confused with each other. Examples could doubtless be found across the whole range of Christian and religious traditions. Fowler[2] however, sets out to analyse the response of Protestant Christians and of "Fundamentalists" in particular, and identifies four main attitudes – namely indifference, hostility, a degree of sympathy for ecological concern, and obsession with "end times." Some dismiss the environmental movement as the prevailing cult of our time, while for others it has apocalyptic dimensions; for others again it represents the anti-Christ, working for world government. One could take issue with such notions, but that must be for another time and place.

---

1 Santmire, *Travail,* 8.
2 Fowler, *Greening.*

Santmire's extensive study shows that there is ambiguity at the heart of the theological tradition of the West, which "is neither ecologically bankrupt … nor replete with immediately accessible, albeit long forgotten, ecological riches hidden everywhere in its deeper vaults"[3]. The ambiguity, he suggests, has been expressed in two quite different trends. One is the notion of the human spirit rising above the mundane level of life in order to commune with God, and the other is to envisage human life as much more embedded in the natural world, and finding God's presence very much within the biosphere. Beyond that, until relatively recent times nature was not perceived as being at risk; the environment was "a given", and ecology as a science was unknown.

The Orthodox scholar Elizabeth Theokritoff has also made a valuable contribution to this discussion, particularly in the way she demonstrates the way in which early Church Fathers such as Irenaeus, Athanasius and others dealt with issues of the material world. One brief example must suffice:

> Irenaeus forcefully emphasizes a truth that the Orthodox Church has never lost sight of: we ourselves are material creatures. We are created as body-and-spirit, and it is as body-and-spirit that we are destined to be saved and transfigured. And this means that in our movement towards Christ, we cannot but bring all creation with us[4].

How "green" is God?

But how "green" is God really? I do not propose to deal with this question at length here, but several basic points must be made. It is one thing to print a version of the Bible in which all the environmental passages are in green ink; but it must be acknowledged that there are less friendly passages, or what Habel describes as "grey texts"[5]; and having named those texts he proceeds to show a way in which they can be read with integrity in our current ecological context. But the point must be made that we do not use the Bible merely as a source of "proof texts"; as we read the Bible so we seek the wisdom to perceive its emphases and to interpret its words faithfully within the context of our

---

3 Santmire, *Travail*, 8

4 Elizabeth Theokritoff, *Living in God's Creation: Orthodox Perspectives on Ecology.* (New York: St Vladimir's Seminary Press, 2009), 42.

5 Norman Habel, *An Inconvenient Text: is a Green Reading of the Bible Possible?* (Adelaide: ATF Press, 2009).

time. So through its pages we may hear a word from God about this world in which we live and our role as one of Earth's creatures.

Playing with Fire

One text that is bound to be cited by those who question or oppose Earth care is 2nd Peter 3 verse 10; why bother caring for the Earth if God is going to burn it up, they ask. I do not propose to deal with this at length, but several points must be made. First, the context of the passage must be noted. The writer is talking about the Day of the Lord and refuting the claims of those who deny the Parousia or Second Coming of Christ. Second, there are variant translations of verse 10. The NRSV translates:

> But the day of the Lord will come like a thief, and then the heavens will pass away with a loud noise, and the elements will be dissolved with fire, and the earth and everything that is done on it will be disclosed.

Note that the preferred translation is "disclosed" or "found", not "burned up". What is at stake here is not some kind of Earth-hating deity, but a God who is concerned about human sinfulness. In other words, this is about purification of the earth and not about destruction. Third, what is foreshadowed is a new heaven and earth; as Watson states, "The new heavens and earth are the home of righteousness, and righteousness will characterize its citizens as well"[6]. Clearly a reading of the text in context offers no joy to those who want an excuse to avoid Earth care.

Dominion or Domination?

An important issue to emerge is the allegation that the Hebrew Bible promotes human domination of the natural environment. But from a biblical point of view, what might be termed the crisis of domination builds on a misunderstanding of Genesis 1:27, in which humankind, both male and female, is created in the image of God: "So God created humankind in his image, in the image of God he created them; male and female he created them" (Gen 1:27). More directly, the misunderstanding is based on a reading of Genesis 1:28, in which "God blessed them, and God said to them, 'Be fruitful and multiply, and fill the earth and subdue it; and have dominion … over every living thing that moves upon the earth". The historian Toynbee is not alone in what I will argue is a misunderstanding of the intention of the

---

6 Duane F Watson, "The Second Letter of Peter" in *The New Interpreters Bible*, Vol 12 (Nashville: Abingdon, 1998), 357.

Genesis text, and thereby potentially turning dominion into an exploitative domination that would need to be repudiated by later texts.

But beyond Toynbee, the Genesis text is not always understood by its critics. For example, many ecofeminists also hold to what I take to be a fundamental misunderstanding of the intent of the Christian faith in relation to the natural environment. A number of these people, including Spretnak, Griffin, Christ, and Grey for example, repudiate Christianity; they hold Christianity in contempt, believing it to be hostile to nature in general and to women in particular. I would argue that what they cite as evidence is in fact based on a failure to grasp the full range of Christian theological understanding, and therefore contributes to the general mis-understanding. As McGrath suggests, there is a movement that holds human liberation and fulfilment as coming through the domination of nature, but it is not Christianity[7].

I referred earlier to White's watershed 1967 essay, "The Historical Roots of our Ecological Crisis", concerning which much has been written over the years, much of it critical. In his essay, White is quite clear that the Christian dogma of creation is largely to blame for the crisis; once again his argument centres on Genesis 1:28, but, I would contend, in an exegetically simplistic manner. It should be acknowledged that some theological expressions have encouraged environmental exploitation; but I argue that these are distortions, and that critics of Christianity, including White, have in fact completely misunderstood the true nature and meaning of dominion.

Biblical Dominion

Genesis 1:28 expresses God's call for humans to "have dominion", which at first may sound environmentally hostile. But when assumptions are set aside and the text is read in context, a different approach emerges. Thus Fretheim states that "a study of the verb *have dominion* (Heb *rada*) reveals that it must be understood in terms of care-giving, even nurturing, not exploitation". We might note that verse 27 reads: "So God created humankind in his image, in the image of God he created them; male and female he created them". In the light of that verse Fretheim's comment is obvious enough: "As the image of God, human beings should relate to the

---

7 McGrath, *Re-enchantment*, 34.

nonhuman creation as God relates to them"[8]. Claus Westermann[9] similarly asserts that dominion is primarily about relationship. In his view it refers to the animal world, and he refutes the notion that dominion should be understood as a mandate for exploitation. For Bradley[10], while dominion may seem to suggest a primacy of humans in the hierarchy of the animal kingdom, in fact the Hebrew *nefesh hayya* indicates that humans are bound together with other living things – animals, birds, fish, and insects. Thus, it is important that the dominion of Genesis 1 needs to be read in the context of God's *shalom*, in the nature of God as expressed in Jesus Christ and the way in which humankind is intended to reflect God's good purpose, rather than a modern industrial society. Moltmann adds an additional point, when in reference to Genesis 1:28, he asserts that "the biblical charge is a dietary commandment: human beings and animals alike are to live from the fruits which *the earth* brings forth in the form of plants and trees. A seizure of power over nature is not intended"[11].

It is important to understand that dominion does not mean domination, but rather that all people are charged with a God-given stewardship; as Calvin DeWitt states, "We have seen from Gen 1-11 what stewardship is not; from Genesis 2:15 we learn something of what it is"[12]. The American Presbyterian Eco Task Group Report[13] focuses strongly on the Genesis 2:15 injunction "to till and keep" the garden. DeWitt and others point out that the Hebrew word for "tend" reflects a strong notion of service, and so he renders the phrase, "to serve and keep" the garden. The Hebrew *"shamar"* (keep) is an extremely rich word with a deeply penetrating meaning that evokes "a loving, caring, sustaining keeping"[14]. Without that critical aspect of care, the concept of the image of God ceases to have any meaning. Indeed, DeWitt is surely correct in his assertion that "dominion as licence

---

8 Terence E Fretheim, *The Book of Genesis.* In "The New Interpreters Bible", Nashville: Abingdon Press, 1994), 346.

9 Westermann, *Creation.*

10 Bradley, *God is Green.*

11 Moltmann, *God in Creation*, 29.

12 Calvin B DeWitt, *Caring for Creation: Responsible Stewardship of God's Handiwork* (Grand Rapids, MI: Barker Book House, 1998), 44.

13 Presbyterian Eco-Justice task Group. 1989. *Keeping and Greening the Creation.* (Louisville, KY: Committee on Social Witness Policy, Presbyterian Church, USA, 1989).

14 DeWitt, *Caring,* 44.

to do whatever meets one's self-interest is a misappropriation of the image of God, and a failure to follow the example of Jesus Christ"[15].

Perhaps enough has been said to project a picture of the biblical understanding of "image" and "dominion"; there is a need to move beyond a belief in creation to an adequate understanding of it.

A Theological Approach

We move then to the important matter of the validity of eco-theology, to see that eco-theology is not only valid, but is indeed part of the mainstream of theology and relates at many levels.

Creation

The Bible begins with the grand affirmation that "In the beginning God created…", and in many ways we also begin at that point. But there is one "red herring" that must be despatched at the outset, and that is the perception that a doctrine of creation is about how the world came to be, or that one must choose between creation and evolution. Put simply, the Bible is not about science or cosmology. There is something more significant involved.

Migliore refers to a new interest in the doctrine of creation, and the reason is located in the environmental crisis. As he states, "… every exposition of the doctrine of God as creator and of the world as God's good creation is profoundly challenged by the ecological crisis"[16]. Further, he says that "The gravity and scope of the ecological crisis give unprecedented urgency to the task of rethinking the Christian doctrine of creation"[17].

Creation represents an affirmation about the world and us. In all its finitude and limitation, creation is good. This is in sharp contrast with a Neo-Platonic dualism that still tends to prevail in some circles; this is the belief that spirit is good and matter is evil, that "earth" equates with "dirty" and from "the world" we move quickly to "the flesh and the devil!" But two brief observations may be in order. First, when John 3:16, e.g., speaks about God loving the world, the Greek word is *kosmos,* which introduces a wider dimension. Second, if the Incarnation says nothing else, it says that "the Word became flesh and dwelt among us, full of grace and truth,"

15 DeWitt, *Caring*, 46.

16 Daniel L Migliore, *Faith Seeking Understanding: an introduction to Christian Theology (2nd ed)*. Grand Rapids: Eerdmans, 2004), 92.

17 Migliore, *Faith Seeking Understanding*, 93.

Creation introduces a broader and deeper dimension to our understanding, and includes not only what we understand as ecology or nature, but also the universe itself. The key is the faith or belief that God created matter and is the source of life, and this is God's world. At the heart of that belief is the concept of *creatio ex nihilo,* that God created everything from nothing. This approach has long been dominant, even though it may not be self-evident from the Genesis text.

Indeed, Young observes that the creation stories were not part of the earliest tradition; rather than beginning with God as 'maker of heaven and earth, the ancient Israelite declarations of faith "began with Abraham and the patriarchs because that is how Israel's experience of God began, and consequently the primary Genesis for Israel was the creation of the people from those who had been no people. That, from their own experience, was *creatio ex nihilo*"[18]. But the doctrine affirms, as Migliore puts it, that "God alone is the source of all that exists"[19], that creation is based on the divine initiative alone. Consequently, Creator and creature are by no means on an equal footing.

Some writers have related creation to *kenosis,* or in other words that creation takes place through a divine withdrawal that leaves space for matter. Brunner, for example, argues that "The kenosis, which reaches its paradoxical climax in the cross of Christ, began with the creation of the world"[20]. But these are difficult ideas to comprehend, and there is a speculative element involved. Thus, *creation ex nihilo* is not merely the belief that God "made everything", but also that God alone is the basis of meaning and value in all things.

As Moltmann states, "The limited sphere of reality which we call 'nature' must be lifted into the totality of being which is termed 'God's creation'"[21]; and that, as Duchrow and Liedke[22] point out, includes an element of relationship with God. It cannot be extended to mean that all societal systems, for example, are God's creation, but rather that all things are subject to divine authority. The concept of creation therefore, as an on-

---

18 Norman Young. *Creator, Creation and Faith.* (London: Collins, 1976), 26.

19 Migliore, *Faith Seeking Understanding*), 100.

20 Cited in Hendrikus Berkhof, *Christian Faith: An Introduction to the Study of Faith.* Grand Rapids: WB Eerdmans Publishing, 1986), 160.

21 Moltmann, *God in Creation,* 21.

22 Duchrow and Liedke, *Shalom.*

going process, adds a new and deeper dimension to the current concern about the future of the planet. What will it mean to be answerable not just to our peers or even our children and grandchildren, but to our God for the quality of our stewardship?

Creation and Redemption

It is essential to recognise that the doctrines of creation and redemption belong together absolutely, and in a Trinitarian framework. The first theologian of note to engage the issues of creation and redemption was Irenaeus, and Brunner is probably correct in regarding him as the key figure in preserving the unity of God as Creator and Redeemer. To see in Jesus Christ the focus of both creation and redemption need not lead to a narrowing of theological scope, but rather, with Christ at the centre, they can be held together in unity.

If a theological unity is to be found, the problem posed by a fall-redemption approach to Christology must be addressed. Treston[23] rightly believes that this has been one of the major issues in the loss of a creation theology. The approach that I am advocating, in line with Treston, begins with God's loving act of creation, or creation as grace, as Karl Barth would affirm; but rather than the Christ event being a "Plan B" effort because of the failure of "Plan A", Christ as Redemptive Word is part of the creative process itself. Christ as Logos links Genesis and John, creation and redemption. Our brokenness, or what some might call Original Sin, is part of us, as an ambivalence of nature, allowing us to move away from God, or by God's grace to allow the *imago Dei* to be realised in us. The Kingdom of God, in the teaching of Jesus, is the basis of God's holistic new creation in the world. Further, Christ's mission was no less than the restoration of harmony in the world, for "in him all things hold together" (Col. 1:17).

At another level we might consider the story of Adam and Eve in the paradise of Eden, in which they were told not to eat of the fruit of the tree of the knowledge of good and evil in the middle of the garden. They disregarded that of course, and so found themselves expelled from their paradise. As Fretheim puts it, "To be separated from the tree of life represents the broken nature of the relationship, with death being inevitable"; he goes

23 Kevin Treston. *Creation Theology: Theology of Creation.* (Samford, Qld: Creation Enterprises, 1990).

on to suggest that "it may be that death (and life) has a comprehensive meaning in this story (as in the Hebrew Scriptures generally) associated with a breakdown in relationships to God, to each other, and to the created order"[24]. That seems to me to be a highly significant observation. In other words what was at stake was not so much that they disobeyed God's law, but rather that they damaged the relationship of trust between God and themselves.

It should not be imagined, however, that redemption was a divine afterthought. Rather, the biblical story is one in which creation and redemption are inexorably related, since redemption in all its dimensions takes place within a world, indeed a universe, that was brought into being through God's grace. Care is needed lest we limit God's purpose too much, either to human concerns exclusively, or to Israel exclusively. As Fretheim observes, "God's purpose in redemption does not, finally, centre on Israel. God as Creator has a purpose that spans the world.... Israel's election furthers God's mission on behalf of the entire universe"[25]. Thus, creation and redemption are both expressions of the one essential reality, which is God's desire for a meaningful relationship with the whole creation, and not least with the human community.

It has not been my purpose here to try to develop this theology fully, but rather to suggest that there is a viable alternative to more traditional approaches that focus on human sinfulness and God's response. This other approach is more positive and less prone to the problem of dualism, since it places Christ, and not our human problems, at the centre. Moltmann adds an important additional element here, in his approach to creation in the Spirit. Creation, he says, is "a Trinitarian process; the Father creates through the Son in the Holy Spirit"[26]. He draws on Psalm 104:29-30 for support:

When you hide your face, they are dismayed;

When you take away their breath, they die and return to their dust.

---

24 Terence E Fretheim. *The Book of Genesis*. In "The New Interpreters Bible", (Nashville: Abingdon Press, 1994), 352.

25 Fretheim. *The Book of Genesis*, 355

26 Moltmann, *God in Creation*, 9.

For Stendahl, that same Psalm is a reminder that "God's Spirit is the breath of life in all creation", and it is wrong "to speak about human dignity in such a manner that we set ourselves up against the rest of creation"[27]. As he notes, in the Genesis accounts we humans did not even rate a day of our own, but had to share it with many other living things! But for Moltmann, the Spirit always means energy: "Everything that is, exists and lives in the unceasing inflow of the energies and potentialities of the cosmic Christ"[28].

My argument is therefore that theologies of creation or of redemption cannot stand in isolation, but are part of the on-going activity of the triune God. Thus, if we experience God as triune, as Creator, Redeemer, and Inspiration, we will see that creation and redemption belong together. More than that, I believe Moltmann is right to maintain[29] that simply to talk about creation and redemption in terms of a "two-term, dual structure," is to miss the important dimension of the Spirit.

Grace

In the light of what has been said, we may safely conclude that creation and grace are inter-related themes. At one level we see that so clearly in the Incarnation, in which God graced our human flesh, when the Almighty became one of us, thus demonstrating that matter matters. More than that, as Migliore puts it, "The grace of God did not first become active in the calling of Abraham or in the sending of Jesus. In the act of creation, God already manifests the self-communicating, other-affirming communion-forming love that defines God's eternal triune reality and that is decisively disclosed in the ministry and sacrificial death of Jesus Christ"[30]. Migliore goes on to describe this act of creation not just as grace but as "costly grace" in the tradition of Bonhoeffer, and in doing so employs Brunner's use of *kenosis* as a way of describing God's action. Thus, creation is perceived as a divine self-emptying, a self limitation that others may have life.

Divine grace is bound to emerge as a crucial insight if we are to understand God, ourselves, and our place on Earth. Jenkins' phrase is "ecologies of grace", and it demonstrates how grace is an undergirding element in the whole discussion of the way faith relates to the Earth. James Nash makes

---

27 K Stendahl. *Energy for Life*. (Geneva: WCC Publications, 1990), 16.
28 Moltmann, *God in Creation*, 9.
29 Moltmann, *God in Creation*, 7.
30 Migliore, *Faith Seeking Understanding*, 101.

a useful contribution when he declares that "the logic of the doctrine of creation does not permit a nature-grace dichotomy"[31]. He shows himself as a disciple of Sittler as he goes on to assert:

> Grace is not only the forgiveness of sins but the 'givenness' of life, both redemption and creation – 'a double gratuity'. The whole of nature – the biophysical universe – is not the antithesis of grace, but rather an expression of grace...

Perhaps more than anyone else in his time, Sittler viewed the whole of creation as an expression of grace, and we need to recapture that sense.

Eucharist

In the light of what has been said thus far, it is important to recognise the relationship between creation care and the centre piece of Christian worship, namely the Eucharist. Denis Edwards draws this out very well in his "Jesus and the Natural World"[32]. The bread and the cup speak to us of the interconnectedness of all life, and of creation and redemption as an act of divine grace. Worshippers have long regarded the sacrament as a celebration of redemption; but that cannot be separated from creation. In bringing the bread and wine, Edwards says, "we symbolically bring the whole creation to the table of God"[33]. Through the act of Communion itself and in being conscious of the ecological implications of some of the prayers we are drawn into a richer experience of God and to what has been called ecological conversion; that of course includes not only a turning from exploitation to Earth-care, but also a respect for other life. As Edwards states, "Fidelity to Christ, fidelity to what we do in the Eucharist, necessarily involves us into fidelity to God's creation, to respect for the integrity of the natural world, to love for the other living creatures of Earth, and to commitment to their wellbeing and flourishing"[34].

Covenant

One of the foremost ways the Bible has of expressing the idea of a divine-human relationship is through the concept of a covenant. The Hebrew

---

31 James Nash. *Loving Nature: Ecological Integrity and Christian Responsibility.* (Nashville: Abingdon, 1991), 95.
32 Denis Edwards, *Jesus and the Natural World: Exploring a Christian Approach to Ecology.* (Mulgrave, Vic: Garratt, 2012).
33 Edwards, *Jesus and the Natural World*, 48.
34 Edwards, *Jesus and the Natural World*, 57.

word underlying this is *chesed,* or the covenant love of God, which builds upon *'ahabah,* which is God's unconditional love for Israel. It is because of this unconditional love for Israel, and thus for all people, that the concept of covenant emerged. At a human level, a covenant carried some of the connotations of a contract between two parties; in this biblical sense, however, it became much more than that, and was required to carry a much greater weight of significance. It is, after all, describing a relationship.

In using the term in this way however, it is important to note that the two parties bound by the covenant are not necessarily equal in status. That is true both at a human level, as for example in the case of a treaty between rival rulers, and in terms of our relationship with God. Almost by definition, the lack of equality between Creator and creature is fundamental to the relationship.

The first time the word "covenant" is used in the Bible relates to Noah in Genesis 6:18, and it has been customary to regard this as the initial covenant which was reaffirmed in later periods. However, Bühlmann contends that the primary covenant is in fact what he calls the Covenant of Creation. He suggests that for too long we have overemphasized the covenant with Abraham, as if it was only then that God became involved in human affairs. Thus, Bühlmann argues that "without the creation account it would be unclear just who *is* the God of Abraham, Isaac, and Jacob, the God of Jesus Christ, the God of all humankind"[35]. At the same time, Bühlmann is quick to point out the limitations of the term "covenant", in that humankind, as a party to the covenant, came into being through the covenant itself. Yet it is also true that this is part of a universal human experience through the very fact of birth.

The other significant covenant to be noted here is with Noah in Genesis 9:8-17, when after the flood the promise of God was reaffirmed. But it must be understood that this was a sovereign act of grace by God; this is very much a divine Covenant. This rather one-sided arrangement is therefore in keeping with the divine initiative of creation itself. But the important point here is that God affirmed a covenant not only with people, but also with "all living creatures". Indeed it would not be too strong to say that the

---

35 Walbert Bühlmann. *The Chosen Peoples.* (Middlegreen, Slough, UK: St Paul Publications, 1982), 11.

earth itself was included. "As for me, I am establishing my covenant with you and your descendants after you, *and with every living creature that is with you….*" Hosea 2:18 reaffirms that inclusive covenant, and specifically indicates that it is between God and all living beings.

We humans have always had a tendency to think of ourselves as somehow above the rest of creation, and that beyond our human relationships nothing really is important. But important though that is, it is even more important to put ourselves in context, in the sense that we are part of God's creation, and the divine concern is for the whole of creation. Fretheim's observation is an important one: "The covenant has significant ecological implications because God has established it with 'all flesh', with birds and animals and the earth itself, even though they are now alienated from human beings"[36].

One of the covenantal implications of humankind's creation in the image of God is that we are thereby called to follow God's lead in caring about all life. One clear lesson we have had to learn from ecology is that species cannot be treated in isolation. More and more we are discovering that different forms of life are inter-connected, and that ecosystems are more complex than we thought. Thus, the ancient story of a covenant relationship between God and all life relates directly with that inter-connection. Green theologians remind us of the important fact that implicit in the covenant is an acceptance of responsibility, and of an involvement in God's will and work in the world. As humans we share in the unity of all creation, but at the same time the special role and responsibility of people made in the image of God is also recognised. The line between life and God centred approaches is often fuzzy, and that is especially evident in the writing of McFague and Reuther, both of whom identify as eco-feminists and Christian theologians.

Rosemary Radford Ruether's theology is far-reaching, and it is easy to distort through brevity. However, her holistic approach to the environment is clear in her understanding of the covenant, "which includes both norms of harmony with the earth and justice in society"[37]. A number of implications emerge from that. First, as I have argued in chapter 2, the wider issue of justice must be an integral part of any eco-theological

---

36 Fretheim. *The Book of Genesis,* 401.
37 Steven Bouma-Prediger, *The Greening of Theology: The Ecological Models of Rosemary Radford Ruether, Joseph Sittler, and Jurgen Moltmann.* (Atlanta Georgia, Scholars Press, 1995), 43.

agenda. Second, Reuther contends that a hierarchical view of the world, with its assumed superiority and inferiority in patterns of domination, is the main cause of oppression, and thus a shift from hierarchy to equality is essential. But the sense of community she proposes does not mean a smothering of all difference. Ruether states: "A covenantal vision of the relation of humans to other life forms acknowledges the special place of humans in this relationship as caretakers, caretakers who did not create and do not absolutely own the rest of life, but who are ultimately accountable for its welfare to the true source of life, God"[38]. Third, as Bouma-Prediger indicates, it should be clear that Reuther's approach "leads ultimately to the conclusion that some radical theological reconstruction is needed", not least in the way God is conceptualised[39]. A significant question with ecological implications is not merely whether one believes in God, but what sort of God one believes in.

Images of God

A number of disparate approaches are either forthright in their advocacy of biocentrism, or tend in this direction, and in many cases their views are significantly influenced by their concepts of God. But equally there are ways of imaging God that have tended to hinder a full appreciation of the place of humankind in the global eco-system, and that have been a significant hindrance in a wider acceptance of a positive ecotheology. It therefore becomes important to consider ways of imaging God that may help or hinder understanding. One issue that becomes very clear – whether or not Moltmann is necessarily correct in his assertion that "an ecological doctrine of Creation implies a new kind of thinking about God"[40] – is that the image we have of God is important.

God as Triune

One important element that must be noted here is the argument that an ecological doctrine of creation relates to the doctrine of the Trinity. This approach is developed strongly by Moltmann. Likewise Peter Scott[41] claims that the modern separation of humanity from nature can be traced to the displacement of the triune God. The current eco-crisis can be located there,

---

38 Ruether, *Gaia and God, 227.*
39 Bouma-Prediger, *Greening,* 50.
40 Moltmann, *God in Creation,* 13.
41 Peter Scott, *A Political Theology of Nature.* Cambridge: Cambridge Univ Press, 2003).

Scott asserts, and so can be healed only from within theology by a revival of a Trinitarian doctrine of creation interlocking with a political philosophy of ecology. In doing this he draws on moderate deep ecology, ecofeminism, and social and socialist ecologies. The movement of the Holy Spirit, he believes, may be viewed as a renewal of fellowship between humanity and nature through ecological democracy.

Bouma-Prediger also believes that theocentrism, or what I prefer to call theistic biocentrism, requires the doctrine of the Trinity. "If the good news is truly good, then we must affirm a view of God that properly emphasizes the community of love that God is: three distinct but inseparable persons indwelling each other in a perfect communion of love"[42]. In a footnote he acknowledges that to speak of three persons is not to speak of three individuals as we understand it today, although I suspect that for many ordinary people it may require more than a footnote to remove the implication of tritheism, and for that reason while the tri-unity of God is basic Christian doctrine with sound ecological implications, great care needs to be taken in the way it is presented.

At the same time, Bouma-Prediger goes on to introduce the important notion of relationship, to assert that "person necessarily implies relationship"[43]. Edwards contributes the idea of "being-in-one-another" as a way of speaking about the Trinity, arguing that "it preserves the diversity and uniqueness of the Three against the tendency to collapse the Trinity into an undifferentiated unity …. or to see God as three separate individuals, as three gods (tritheism)"[44]. The concept of diversity in unity and the insight that "God's being is a communion of mutual love" therefore serves to emphasise what Moltmann, Borg and others also stress, namely the fundamental value of relationship; or as Edwards states, "the very *being* of things in our universe is relational being"[45]. Such an understanding of God and reality as essentially relational cannot coexist with attitudes of exploitation and domination, whether in the human community, in regard to animal life, or indeed the Earth itself.

---

42 Bouma-Prediger, *Beauty*, 120.
43 Bouma-Prediger, *Beauty*, 203.
44 Denis Edwards, *Ecology at the Heart of Faith: The Change of Heart that leads to a New Way of Living on Earth.* (Maryknoll, New York: Orbis Books, 2006), 72.
45 Edwards, *Ecology*, 76.

Thus, Moltmann rejects a mechanistic approach in which things are primary, and argues that relationships are just as primal – that "to be alive means existing in relationship with other people and things"[46]. Such a view may readily be developed and sustained biblically, and has implications for an understanding of God. In this regard it is important to understand, as we said earlier, that from a biblical perspective the God of Creation is also the God of Redemption.

God and Gender

A number of points begin to emerge very clearly. First, the language we use about God is both problematic and important. The question of gender language and God is important in the context of eco-theology. For many people, the common use of male language for God is not intended to say that God is in fact male, yet even by default that becomes the perception. The question is how we may have a form of language that does justice not only to the biblical record, but also to issues of intimacy and relationship, and at the same time is inclusive yet manageable in common use.

Elizabeth Achtemeier acknowledges that women have a legitimate cause for concern on the grounds of discrimination, but she sees a big difference between "feminism as fairness and feminism as ideology"; for Achtemeier, the latter is seen in attempts to feminise the names of God. Thus, she asserts that a basic principle is involved, in that "The Bible uses masculine language for God because that is the language with which God has revealed himself"[47]; apart from several examples of simile, God is not defined in feminine terms. Rather, God is defined as the God and Father of our Lord Jesus Christ. But that is not to suggest that God is male; rather, for Achtemeier, "the God of the Bible has no sexuality"[48]. It is clear though that Achtemeier's main problem is with those whom she regards as "radical feminists".

Somewhat in contrast to Achtemeier, Paul R. Smith's book from the unlikely background of the Southern Baptist tradition in the United States, asks *"Is it Okay to Call God 'Mother'?: Considering the Feminine Face of God."* His verdict is decisive. God is not incarnate in either gender or language, but in Jesus Christ; but he goes on to state his thesis: "Calling God 'Father' and

---

46 Moltmann, *God in Creation*, 3.
47 Elizabeth Achtemeier, *Nature, God, and Pulpit.* (Grand Rapids, Mich: WB Eerdmans Pub, 1993), 19.
48 Achtemeier, *Nature,* 18.

never 'Mother' says something in our day that Jesus never intended, namely, that God is exclusively male or masculine"[49]. As he develops his argument, he makes the point that "we cannot avoid male and female words because the sense of what is personal for humans only comes in those two forms"[50].

Gail O'Day also makes an important contribution to this debate about gender and God in her introduction to a commentary on John's gospel. In it she notes that the use of male images for God is difficult for many women because of the implications of patriarchy. Many eco-feminists would agree with O'Day that "an exclusive use of father language for God both flattens the richness of biblical images for God that sends disturbing messages about systems of power and authority"[51]. Yet, O'Day argues, we may not remove the Father/Son language of John without seriously distorting his whole theological vision: "The Church's task is to move beyond the assumption that *Father* is a generic synonym for 'God' ... John does not use Father/Son language to reinforce the claims of patriarchy. Rather, he uses it to highlight the theological possibilities of intimacy and love that rest at the heart of God"[52].

Beyond a Monarchical God

Second, McFague is undoubtedly correct in her observation that "the monarchical model, the relation of God and the world in which the divine, all-powerful king controls his subjects and they in turn offer him loyal obedience, is the oldest and still the most prevalent one"[53], and that this model has political implications. I am sure that many would agree with that perception of God as the monarchical male ruler of people. Marcus Borg joins McFague and others in rejecting this model, and in doing so points to a number of implications of this approach. It implies a "radical separation" of God from nature, and that separation of the world from the sacred results in a downgrading of nature. Further, it reinforces notions of dominion and anthropocentrism, leading to the conclusion that "nature has instrumental value, not intrinsic value"[54]. Borg goes on to assert that such a monarchical

---

49 Paul R Smith, 1993. *Is it Okay to Call God "Mother": Considering the Feminine Face of God.* (Peabody, Mass.: Hendrickson Publishers, 1993), 3.

50 Smith, *Is it Okay*, 99.

51 Gail R O'Day, *The Gospel of John*. In *New Interpreters Bible, Vol 9,* (Nashville: Abingdon Press, 1995), 496.

52 O'Day, *The Gospel of John*, 496.

53 McFague, *Body*, 139.

54 Marcus J Borg, *The God we Never Knew.* (San Francisco: HarperCollins, 1997), 68.

concept of God goes hand in hand with an oppressive political system to which it gives legitimacy. Such a correlation of a monarchical view of God and societal structures has inevitable implications for gender issues in a male dominated society.

After considering a monarchical view, Borg helpfully proposes what he calls a "Spirit model" of God which gives a radically different and more holistic meaning to some traditional concepts. In this understanding, primacy is given to "relationship, intimacy and belonging"[55]. Drawing on the Bible itself, Borg projects images of God as Mother, Intimate Father, Lover, and Journey Companion, in addition to a number of non-anthropomorphic metaphors.

A Panentheistic God

Third, there is considerable agreement in the literature that the biblical God is panentheistic, a word that literally means "everything in God", and which should not be confused with the more familiar but completely different term "pantheism". A traditional view would picture God as "wholly other", or what might be described as theism of radical transcendence in which God is pictured totally beyond humankind and the mundane. But the image of God as transcendent is only part of the story. As Borg suggests, panentheism also perceives God as "*the encompassing Spirit* in whom everything that is, is. The universe is not separate from God, but *in* God"[56]. McFague projects a very similar image, which she believes "makes sense" in terms of an incarnational understanding of Christianity and an organic interpretation of modern science[57]. Moreover, she develops that approach in terms of "the body of God". In *Models of God*, for example, McFague tries to re-conceptualise God as Lover, Friend, and Mother, in ways that may transform Christian assumptions and prejudices. Ecological implications are evident in her view of "the world as God's body, which God – and we – mother, love, and befriend. God is incarnated or embodied in our world, in both cosmological and anthropological ways"[58].

Thus, the biblical God is both transcendent and immanent; or as Borg puts it, the terms reflect the "moreness" and the "presence" of God[59]. A biblical

55 Borg, *The God we Never Knew*, 71.
56 Marcus J Borg, *The Heart of Christianity*. (San Francisco: HarperCollins, 2003), 66.
57 McFague, *Body of God*, 150.
58 Sallie McFague, *Models of God: Theology for an Ecological, Nuclear Age*. (Philadelphia: Fortress Press, 1987), 184.
59 Borg, *The Heart*, 66.

example would be Isaiah 6:1, in which the prophet begins to describe his call. In his vision, he sees the Lord "sitting on a throne, high and lofty", yet "the hem of his robe filled the temple". The wonder of the natural world and our sense of God are linked.

Creation Spirituality

It is clear that if theology is going to connect with mission in a practical sense, the development of a nature or creation spirituality will be quite essential. A number of strands converge at this point, and potentially it opens up a large subject. One possible beginning point may be for humankind to heed the call of the late Pope John Paul II to emulate the example of Francis of Assisi, and "make peace with all of creation[60].

But a form of creation spirituality in fact reaches far back into Church history. Here the name of Matthew Fox comes readily to mind, drawing as he does on Meister Eckhart (1260-1327) and other medieval theologians and mystics. It is very clear that there is a profound mysticism at the heart of Fox's approach. There is much that could be said here, but clearly a perspective which recognises both God's "moreness" and nearness is basic; from that point, many other issues emerge, from experience to a positive view of faith and science, and from compassion to an appreciation of the natural world. One may disagree with Fox on some theological issues; but to perceive with him that "the mystic in us is the one moved to radical amazement by the *awe* of things"[61] is to realise that such an approach has significant implications not only for human relationships with God, but also for creation care.

McFague, for whom God is "sacramentally embodied", is one who makes a similar connection: "The world is our meeting place with God ... as the body of God, it is wondrously, awesomely, divinely mysterious"[62]. However, she critically evaluates the work of Thomas Berry and Matthew Fox. In doing so, she states, "creation spirituality has given the planetary agenda a number of key insights necessary for cosmic health"[63]. At its best, she says, it provides "a mystique of the earth"; or in the words of Berry, "the universe,

---

60 Pope John Paul 11, *Peace with God the Creator, Peace with all of Creation.* Australian ed., (Homebush, NSW: St Paul Publications, 1990).

61 Matthew Fox, *The Coming of the Cosmic Christ.* (North Blackburn, Vic.: Collins Dove, 1988), 51.

62 McFague, *Body of God*, vii.

63 McFague, *Body of God*, 70.

by definition, is a single gorgeous celebratory event"[64]. Thus, McFague is happy to affirm the positives that she perceives in creation spirituality. It evokes a sense of deep appreciation of and connection with the Earth, which influences the way we act.

However, she takes Berry and Fox to task for their failure to acknowledge the negative side as well. For McFague, they lack "a sense of the awful oppression that is part and parcel of the awesome mystery and splendour"[65]. Thus, their approach contains an unfounded optimism. In more precise terms, for example, she is critical of Fox for his omission of repentance and his neglect of North-South social justice issues. Nevertheless, for McFague, creation spirituality is "a utopian, eschatological vision and ought to be allowed to function in that way"[66]. Certainly it does not project reality as it is, but in a prescriptive rather than a descriptive sense, it has an important contribution to make to the planetary care agenda.

Norman Habel has also made a significant contribution to our under-standing of creation spirituality through his book "Rainbow of Mysteries". Habel's approach focuses on the "Rainbow Covenant" of Genesis 9 and thus associates each of the seven colours with a particular mystery. The rationale in choosing the rainbow paradigm is obvious: "The rainbow served to remind God of God's bond and divine connection with Earth and all of creation. My rainbow, following the precedent of the Creator, represents my covenant promise to explore my bonds with Earth, my spiritual connections with creation"[67]. This is an enriching personal journey which the reader is invited to take time to explore.

Perhaps enough has been said to highlight the enormous significance of spirituality for any praxis of creation care. McFague expresses that link clearly when she states that "piety and praxis go together"[68]; but for both Ruether and McFague, as indeed for others such as Deane-Drummond, there is a strong link between human attitudes to nature and consequences, so that creation spirituality involves a committed love of nature as a central

---

64 Berry, *Dream*, 5.

65 McFague, *Body of God*, 72.

66 McFague, *Body of God*, 72.

67 Norman Habel, *Rainbow of Mysteries*. (Kelowna Canada, CooperHouse (Wood Lake Publishing) 2012), 17.

68 Sallie McFague, *Super, Natural Christians: How we should love nature*. (London: SCM Press, 1997), 11.

driving force. Ruether expressed that clearly when she stated, "What we need is neither optimism nor pessimism but committed love"[69]. But McFague deals with the kind of understanding that must underlie such a love. For her, this love begins by seeing nature as subject rather than as object: "Christians should not only be natural, understanding ourselves as *in* and *of* the earth, but also super, natural, understanding ourselves as excessively, superlatively concerned with nature and its well-being"[70]. She goes on to point out that loving nature, which is what is required, depends on careful attention to it, *"because we cannot love what we do not know"*[71]. McFague's use of italics emphasises the importance of the point. Ruether's summing up of the implications is helpful: it means that "we remain committed to a vision and to concrete communities of life, no matter what the 'trends' may be. After all, it is for our children and for generations of living beings to come"[72].

Conclusion

In this chapter I have addressed some critical issues including the question "how green is God?", dominion versus domination and Santmire's assertion of the ambiguous ecological heritage of theology. I have considered a number of theological doctrines, especially a doctrine of creation as it relates not only to redemption and grace, but also to the Eucharist; that in turn has led to the significant biblical image of covenant and what that says about the place of human life and responsibility.

I have considered some of the ways in which God is understood, such as the significance of a Trinitarian understanding, the issue of gendered language, and leading on to an image of God who is both transcendent and immanent, or what has been termed a panentheistic view which I have suggested is both true to the biblical record and also helpful in terms of eco-theology. There are many theological elements with inherent implications for transformation and renewal; this is reflected in the importance of creation spirituality in which piety and praxis are shown to belong together. The significance of that link and of the issues raised in this chapter will be shown to be fundamentally important in terms of the ecological responses and theology of eco-mission that will be developed in the next chapter.

---

69 Ruether, *Gaia and God*, 273.
70 McFague, *Super Natural Christian*, 6.
71 McFague, *Super Natural Christian*, 29.
72 Ruether, *Gaia and God*, 273.

CHAPTER FIVE

Towards an Eco-mission Theology

Like any form of theology, eco-theology comes in a variety of forms ranging from a position close to deep ecology to a stance that is totally human-centred. Similarly it will not be surprising to find that in terms of mission, a Christian response to the natural environment also draws a variety of different expressions; nor should that be considered a problem. But at the outset it is clear that Christian mission must be more than mere pragmatism; a Christian response is bound to emerge directly from the primary theology that shapes it. If exploitative approaches are set aside, a valid theology and praxis of eco-mission can emerge out of a range of theologies.

The best known response is stewardship, but it is not the only one, and it is not without its critics. Other responses are captured by rubrics such as partnership, Earth community, sacrament, covenant, celebration, and even pastoral care. Thus the purpose of this chapter is to consider these responses and how they might relate to one another; the question of whether the differences are real or more a matter of semantics will be explored. One issue that will emerge quite quickly is that there is a considerable amount of overlap between them, and thus I will be arguing for a new composite model or response.

There are, however, a number of primary theological questions in behind the various possible eco-mission models. For example, how is "dominion" to be defined? What is the status or relationship of humankind with the natural world? I have considered these and other questions in previous chapters; but differences at the mission level rise out of legitimately different answers to those primary questions, or differing assumptions about or even outright misunderstanding of the meaning of key words. In this chapter we will look at six possible responses to eco-theology before going on to consider ways of defining mission, and finally attempting a basic theology of eco-mission.

Dominion

Rasmussen begins his analysis with what he calls the dominion model, which he clearly regards as out of place today, although it is doubtful if this is valid as a stand-alone approach. For dominion, as Rasmussen defines it, is not the Genesis text-in-context version, but rather the distortion better described as domination. He asserts that "commerce masquerading as human liberation is not the only surviving form of dominion theology, but it is the most prominent one"[1]. I do not intend to revisit the issue here; I have previously argued that in real terms dominion has little to do with human mastery and control, and that dominion understood as domination has little that is positive to say to the current eco-crisis. But a dominion theology understood in terms of its serving nature, or as a reflection of the spirit of Christ is another matter, and will be part of at least some of the responses that follow. As Fowler observes, dominion understood in that sense "does not deny stewardship but requires it"[2].

Stewardship

For some people, stewardship emerges as the most obvious descriptor of the human relationship with the natural world. Thus Hart[3] is not obviously aware of the debate surrounding the term "stewardship", which he appears to regard as uncontroversial, and consequently he does not argue the case for it. In his writing and in citing the declarations of Councils of Catholic Bishops Hart clearly regards stewardship as the normative term to describe our human place and role in creation.

Compared with the other responses, however, there is a great deal of literature concerning stewardship, with scholars lined up on both sides of the debate. Thus, at the outset it is important to note Fowler's observation that stewardship comes in many versions, even though there may be some common themes such as the image of God as "the sacred Creator" and nature as God's creation[4]. What becomes clear in the debate is that one's final position tends to depend to a large extent on the prior assumptions or understandings one brings to it; it means that the approach the critics of stewardship reject often does not correspond with the approach that its proponents affirm.

On the one hand, for the Au Sable Institute and Calvin DeWitt, stewardship clearly means the bringing of healing and wholeness not

1 Larry L Rasmussen, *Earth Community, Earth Ethics*. (Geneva: WCC Publications, 1996), 229.
2 Fowler, *Greening*, 81
3 Hart, *What are they Saying*.
4 Fowler, *Greening*, 76-7.

only to the biosphere but indeed to the whole of Creation. DeWitt asserts that stewardship "addresses the problems at their roots", and thus "is not crisis management but a way of life"[5]. Similarly, a Report commissioned by the Anglican Church's Mission and Public Affairs Council asserts that "the biblical term for humanity's relationship with creation is 'steward'", understood in terms of a dominion "under God" and exercised on God's behalf, and of accountability to God for "tilling and keeping"[6]. And from a rather different orientation, Berry cites a UK Government White Paper in 1990 which asserts that "the ethical imperative of stewardship ... must underlie all (government) environmental policies"[7]. The Paper goes on to define stewardship as the "duty to look after our world prudently and conscientiously". The fact that the term "stewardship" is contained in a Government White Paper may serve at least as a question mark over Scott's concern that the term is too entrenched in ecclesial imagery to communicate effectively in the public arena beyond the Church.

On the other hand, much of the opposition to the notion of stewardship rises out of a fundamentally different definition, and centres on several related perceptions. From a philosophical orientation, for example, Passmore[8] is sceptical not only about the stewardship tradition, which he regards as relatively weak, but also about the role of Christianity in general. A second area of opposition is based on historical considerations. Roderick Nash[9] not only rejects stewardship, but also the assertion that it has had an honoured place in Christian history. For him, there is scant historical evidence to support a positive assessment. As Nash sees it, stewardship was totally absent for 1,000 years after Benedict in the 6th century, and only re-appeared in relatively recent times. He clearly brings a type of deep ecological understanding as expressed in an implied sympathy for the smallpox virus.

---

5 DeWitt, *Caring for Creation*, 47.

6 Anglican Church Mission and Public Affairs Council, 2005, 26.

7 RJ Berry, *God's Book of Works: The Nature and Theology of Nature*. (London & New York: T & T Clark, 2003), 183.

8 John Passmore, *Man's Responsibility for Nature: Ecological Problems and Western Traditions*. (London: Duckworth, 1974).

9 Roderick Nash, *The Rights of Nature: A History of Environmental Ethics*. (Leichhardt NSW: Primavera Press, 1990).

The most significant focus of opposition is the perception that stewardship is based on human supremacy and exploitation. Hallman, for example, who is committed to creation care, believes that the current trend in eco-theology is away from a theology of stewardship, and his reason is clear. He believes that stewardship is based on the notion of human supremacy, and adds, "even if now we talk more in terms of human responsibility than dominion, our approach is still a management model *in which we humans think we know best*" (italics mine)[10]. There are several problems with this. It certainly recalls the earlier debate about "dominion", and it is doubtful if it is a fair reflection of the care that underlies the thinking of those who support stewardship. In any event one could ask if we could do anything other than what we believe is best.

Primavesi and Northcott take the argument further when they introduce a profit motive. Thus, for Primavesi, stewardship remains "exploitative and unecological, since the stewards seek to optimise profits for themselves or their bosses"[11]. This is related to her objection to what she perceives as "hierarchical thinking", or the idea that humans are somehow "above" or "in charge of" the ecosystem, and thus that stewardship is about the ultimate benefit to humankind. Northcott likewise regards stewardship as highly problematic, and the reason, in part, is that he sees it as based strongly on anthropocentrism, and seems unconvinced by the argument that "dominion" does not involve "a purely instrumentalist vision of nature which legitimates ecological plunder". I would argue that Northcott exaggerates the human factor in the stewardship model in his perception that it infers an ordering of other life to meet the needs of human life. My contention is that Northcott has not really understood what many proponents of stewardship are advocating.

The most immediate and obvious response to such criticisms is that it all depends on how the stewards' job description is written. Certainly it is not difficult to find examples of poor stewardship; but the perception of stewardship as essentially exploitative is not supported in the writing of those who advocate stewardship.

---

10 DG Hallman ed. *Ecotheology: Voices from South and North.* Geneva, (WCC Publications, and New York: Orbis Books, 1994), 6.

11 Anne Primavesi, *From Apocalypse to Genesis: Ecology, Feminism, and Christianity* (Minneapolis; Tunbridge Wells, Kent: Fortress press; Burns and Oates, 1991), 107.

Thomas Derr presents a credible response to the criticisms of Northcott, Hallman, and others. Derr has problems with biocentrism, and frankly embraces the term anthropocentrism as a reflection of the *imago Dei;* thus, Derr's position is similar to DeWitt's, and in the mould of Calvin, when he states, "I would stress again ... that we are made to cultivate and manage the earth, not passively accept whatever nature brings". The term he uses is "managerial stewardship"[12]. The key for Derr is Genesis 2:15 and the divine call to "tend the earth and keep it"; as he puts it, "dominion as licence to do whatever meets one's self-interest is a misappropriation of the image of God, and a failure to follow the example of Jesus Christ"[13].

D.J. Hall was one of the first to advocate stewardship as a particularly appropriate metaphor for a Christian response to creation, but this is a position that can only be reached after it has taken seriously the criticism levelled against the ecological legacy of the Christian faith. Hall rejects the view that humanity is "above nature" as if possessed of some innate superior endowments, and in reaching that view he considers the concept of *imago Dei.* "But if the image of God does not refer to a quality that we possess (making us superior to other creatures), but to a relationship in which we stand vis-a vis our Creator, and a vocation to which we are called within the creation, a very different conception of the humankind-otherkind relation follows"[14], and he locates the image of steward in such a context. Further, he scornfully rejects the notion of humanity "in nature" as a naïve position. The key for Hall is the notion of humanity "with nature", considered against the background of what it means to "have dominion".

Thus, to "have dominion" requires that "we should be servants, keepers and priests in relation to the others"[15], and we can only fulfil that representative role if we are not only different from "otherkind", but also in some sense the same as they are. The significance of such an understanding is that contrary to the understanding of critics of the term, stewardship implies accountability to God and a special responsibility to care for the earth and

---

12 Thomas S Derr, *The Complexity and Ambiguity of Environmental Stewardship.* Response in Calvin B DeWitt, "Caring for Creation: Responsible Stewardship of God's Handiwork". (Grand Rapids, MI: Barker Book House, 1998), 82.
13 Derr, *Complexity*, 46.
14 Douglas John Hall, 2006. *Stewardship as Key to a Theology of Nature.* In R.J. Berry (ed) "Environmental Stewardship". (London and New York: T & T Clark, 2006), 137.
15 Hall, *Stewardship*, 142.

other creatures. Thus, for Hall it becomes an apt symbol and basis for an ecological ethic. But as Macquarrie cautions, "Man is tempted to move from being guardian of the world to becoming its exploiter, from use to reckless abuse. He forgets that he is also a creature and must have respect for nature's laws"[16].

The 1994 *Evangelical Declaration on the Care of Creation*[17] is a deeply spiritual and caring document based on the stewardship model. It acknowledges that our stewardship is flawed, and urges Christians and Churches to be "centres of creation's care and renewal"[18]. Berry's edited volume focussing on the Declaration is interesting in that it includes articles that are mildly critical of it. A case in point is Bauckham's essay, "Stewardship and Relationship"[19], in which he acknowledges the intention of the Declaration to interpret dominion in terms of a caring stewardship, and that it therefore has a "biblical ring" to it. He is bound to note, however, that historically the term "dominion" implied that "the rest of creation exists for human benefit"[20]. It may be noted here that this is not Baukham's own view, but rather his *perception* of the way in which others have understood dominion.

Bauckham's conclusion is to wonder if images such as stewardship or garden are entirely adequate for the use to which they are put in the *Declaration*, and if stewardship "does not come to us still too freighted with the baggage of the modern project of technological domination of nature"[21]. More than that, he identifies at least part of the problem with stewardship as being the image it projects of a purely 'vertical' relationship with the natural world, with humans set above the rest of creation. The 'horizontal' relationship, he suggests, is also important. Given his perception of what stewardship implies, and the potential for abuse, Bauckham avers that "the concept of stewardship itself certainly cannot do all the work of radically reorientating our attitudes to the rest of creation that urgently needs to be done"[22]. The

---

16 Macquarrie, *Principles*, 232.
17 R J Berry, ed. *The Care of Creation: Focusing Concern and Action.* (Leicester: Inter-Varsity Press, 2000), 18-22.
18 Berry, *Care*, 21.
19 Berry, *Care*, 99.
20 Berry, *Care*, 100.
21 Berry, *Care*, 103.
22 Berry, *Care*, 105.

question remains as to whether or not he is correct, and whether any concept alone is able to bear that weight.

A great deal therefore depends on how key words are understood and applied, and thus the lack of an agreed definition is central to the differences in outlook regarding stewardship. But the areas of divergence are critically important, and the variation in understanding needs to be taken into account in attempting to define stewardship. More than that, it is out of this divergence that most of the difficulties emerge.

Partnership

Rightly or wrongly, there is a perception that the stewardship model is anthropocentric and hierarchical in character. By contrast the partnership approach perceives humankind much more as part of creation. Nevertheless, it is still best understood as a variation on the more common stewardship model.

As I noted previously, Bradley is one of a number of writers to focus on the foundational unity of creation, that "at its deepest level the universe is a single unified whole, indivisible, and bound together by a simple yet powerful force"[23]. Thus it is possible to trace the link between humans and other life through the biblical images, such as *adam* (man) and *adama* (ground), and in other passages. Bradley's point is that this position steers a middle course between human domination of nature on the one hand, and the opposite extreme that humans are inferior to nature.

But partnership does not negate the concept of human uniqueness; rather it relocates humans in relationship with the rest of creation. As Hill puts it, "Humankind is partner to otherkind as, in Stephen Jay Gould's phrase, 'the stewards of life's continuity on Earth'"[24]. As some biocentrists would assert more forcefully, other life also has a claim to moral consideration. Rasmussen asserts that it is important to recognise human power in the midst of creation; nevertheless, "the recentered human partner recognises that, whatever power we wield as a species, we do not legislate the laws of an encompassing nature"[25].

---

23 Bradley, *God is Green*, 19.
24 Brennan Hill, *Christian Faith and the Environment: making vital connections.* (Maryknoll, NY: Orbis Books, 1998), 236.
25 Rasmussen, *Earth*, 237.

It may be argued that in pointing to continuity between humankind and otherkind, rather than a radical discontinuity, the partnership model is on solid ground both biblically and scientifically.

Covenant

The covenant approach has its origin in Genesis 9:11-13, in which God establishes a covenant not just with Noah, but also with "every living creature" and the earth itself. "I have set my bow in the clouds, and it shall be a sign of the covenant between me and the earth" (Gen 9:13). The repetition of key words and phrases emphasises both the divine promise itself and its inclusive nature. Again, as noted earlier, Fretheim is surely correct in his assertion that "the covenant has significant ecological implications because God has established it with 'all flesh'", which means that because God cares for non-human life, "human beings should follow the divine lead"[26]. It is noteworthy that the covenant theme is picked up again in Hosea 2:18, which introduces a prophetic theme.

In his summary of options, Rasmussen links "covenant" with "prophet", and notes that those who take this approach tend to be much more interested in a prophetic call for change to save a threatened planet than in metaphysics. The World Council of Churches Program for Justice, Peace, and the Integrity of Creation was based strongly on a covenant theme, and indeed became part of the title of the final document. The document stated that "the integrity of creation has a social aspect which we recognize as peace with justice, and an ecological aspect which we recognise in the self-renewing, sustainable character of natural eco-systems"[27]. Northcott is clearly one who believes the covenant model has more to offer than stewardship. This is due in part to his understanding that stewardship generally relates to instrumentalist and exploitative attitudes to the natural world, but also the perception that "covenant" is more inclusive in character: "The covenant is not simply between humans and God, as anthropocentric exegetes have traditionally held, but is rather a 'cosmic covenant' involving all the orders of creation and linking them with the rituals, ethics and society of humans"[28]. It is clear

---

26 Fretheim, *The Book of Genesis*, 401.

27 D Preman Niles, ed. 1992. *Between the Flood and the Rainbow: Interpreting the Conciliar Process of Mutual Commitment (Covenant) to Justice, Peace and the Integrity of Creation.* (Geneva: WCCPublications, 1992), 174.

28 Northcott, *Environment*, 168.

however that this concept of covenant crosses the usual theological and ecclesiological boundaries.

A number of points emerge from this. First, it is impossible to read the covenant text and assert that humans are "above" the rest of creation. In company with other life, we belong to the earth. There is an important proviso, however. While affirming that fundamental principle, it is entirely possible and appropriate to argue that within the created order of which we are part, there is room for a special relationship between God and humans. I would argue that this is not anthropocentrism, nor does it support a notion of human mastery; it represents a unique relationship and responsibility while remaining part of that "web of life" that God has created. McFague is particularly successful in establishing that balance. As I indicated previously, she affirms both unity and diversity, and acknowledges the inclusive nature of the covenant with Noah. She argues, correctly in my view, that the crucial difference between humans and other life is an awareness of the common creation story; it is that which provides the basis of a strong environmental ethic, and the paradigm that is needed for responding to other life.

Second, it becomes clear that the covenant/prophet model does not necessarily stand alone, but is incorporated as part of other approaches. McDonagh, for example, clearly projects the stewardship model; but having elaborated briefly on a biblical view of dominion and the Genesis 9 covenant, goes on to assert that an inclusive covenant is at the heart of stewardship. Similarly, the Anglican document *Sharing God's Planet* openly assumes a stewardship paradigm. We are "stewards of creation", a heading declares[29]. But in asking how this stewardship might be exercised, the Report proposes four theological principles, the first of which is the covenant with creation. In my view the Report expresses very well both the inter-connectedness of life and the place of humans within that creation. "The covenant with creation is the acknowledgment of the total interdependence and connectedness of every part of the creation, brought forth from the one God. Humanity stands apart from the rest of creation in this respect: it can understand this relationship, and can express it and renew it in the form of love"[30].

---

29 Anglican Church, *Sharing God's Planet*, 16.
30 Anglican Church, *Sharing God's Planet*, 19.

Sacrament

The sacrament paradigm is another model with support in sections of the Church, and not least in the Orthodox tradition. But it may be expressed in a number of different ways. McFague, for example, discusses Christian sacramentalism under the heading "Nature and the Cosmic Christ", and declares "the world in our model is the sacrament of God, the visible, physical, bodily presence of God"[31]. This is not dissimilar from Fox's position, and it is one with which some Christians may be uneasy, in that they may feel it is stretching the meaning of "sacrament" too much. It is of note however that in the 16th century Bruno advocated the notion of "a dynamic universe akin to that envisioned by the process philosophers of today"[32]. This extended to the concept of the earth, along with other astronomical bodies, being regarded as a living being. Thus, there are some common elements in Bruno, McFague's "body of God", and the concept of Gaia.

Louw, however, sees this approach as helpful, and notes with approval McFague's description of her "body of God" imagery as panentheism[33]. Rasmussen similarly regards panentheism as an alternate term for sacramentalism. McFague herself cautions that her concept should not be read literally, but rather as analogy and metaphor, and that in adopting a panentheistic stance she is projecting both the transcendence and the immanence of God. At the same time it must be noted that panentheism is almost a universally held position in ecotheology, and so it is potentially quite misleading to link it exclusively with a sacramental approach.

A sacramental approach does not emerge strongly in Gregorios' "Orthodox view of Nature"; much of it is historical and descriptive in character. But he does offer a significant observation: "Humanity has a special vocation as the priest of creation, as the mediator through whom God manifests himself to creation and redeems it. But this does not make humanity totally discontinuous with creation, since a priest has to be an integral part of the people he represents"[34]. For Sherrard, the significance of the priestly metaphor is that, as mediator, humankind is intended to offer the world to

---

31 McFague, *Body of God*, 182.
32 Gregorios, *Human Presence*, 32.
33 DJ Louw, *Dreaming the Land in Hope: towards a practical theological ecclesiology of cura terrae*. Unpublished paper delivered in Brisbane, 2005.
34 Gregorios, *Human Presence*, 85.

God in praise and worship; but because of the Fall, alienation from the Christ "manifests itself in a particularly dehumanising and ecologically destructive form in the culture of modern science"[35]. Northcott himself, like Gregorios, is much more aware of the positive aspects of science and technology. The metaphor of "priest of creation" is therefore somewhat ambiguous in character. Perhaps the key is in Gregorios' reference to Christ's self-denying love, and humankind's need to offer ourselves and the universe to God in love. As he suggests, "the mastery of nature must be held within the mystery of worship. Otherwise we lose both mastery and mystery"[36].

A Composite Model

How then does one begin to pull together the strands of these various models? I contend that the various models are in fact not as different as the labels suggest, that no single word or concept can carry the weight required of it, and that a composite model is not only possible but is indeed essential. As was amply illustrated in the opposing views of stewardship, a great deal depends on how a word is defined, or what content is ascribed to a particular model.

If there is debate about the public, non-Church acceptability of a term like stewardship, the difficulty is exacerbated in the other possibilities. The primary problem with partnership, covenant, sacrament, and pastoral care is not at the content level, but in the fact that these are very much "in-house", ecclesial terms and thus are ill equipped for general use. In terms of a practical theology it may be argued that it probably does not matter very much what label we use, provided we are sure about the substance behind the label. Further, we might ask to what extent we can afford the luxury of the sometimes-excessive semantics of academic debate!

In spite of legitimate reservations about stewardship as the vehicle for creation care, my proposal is for a composite model based on the term "stewardship", but that incorporates the following essential factors, noting that these are not alternatives inviting us to pick and choose.

1. It will reflect a dominion (as distinct from domination) theology based on the *imago Dei* and the servant spirit of Christ.

2. It will express ecological stewardship in terms of partnership; that

---

35 Sherrard cited in Northcott, *The Environment*, 131.
36 Gregorios, *Human Presence*, 89.

is, with humankind seen as part of creation rather than above it and recognising fully the value of other life for its own sake, yet recognising also a special relationship with God and ecological responsibility under God.

3. It will express the biblical language of caring for creation.

4. It will clearly be based on the inclusive covenant of God as expressed to Noah.

5. A panentheistic view of God that sees God as both transcendent and immanent will issue in a sacramental element, but without resorting to the extreme of pantheism.

6. It will recognise the validity of ecological care as an extension of holistic pastoral care.

I have argued that the various models projected in the literature can not legitimately be viewed as in competition with each other, and that a composite model is required. Further, it is doubtful if any one word can be sufficient, and so there needs to be greater emphasis on content, and perhaps a little more charity as well! At the same time, while noting the difficulties, a "flagship" word is required that can to some degree express, for both the Christian community and a wider public, the ecological commitment that is increasingly essential. In that regard, the dominant concept of stewardship, understood in composite terms, is probably the most adequate of the existing possibilities, and its use in a UK Government White Paper provides a hint of a possible wider acceptance. If it can be received without "baggage", it may be possible to infuse into it the various ingredients of a new holistic composite model of eco-mission.

James Nash may have the final word: "Yet, perhaps the bottom line is this: the strict constructionists and sectarians who yearn for ideological and verbal purity in the environmental movement do well to pay less attention to words and more to values and commitments. They might find a fair number of allies, including among those 'unregenerates' who are content with *conservation, stewardship,* or even *dominion*"[37].

Towards Mission

I have outlined a number of theological approaches to ecology and the natural world, and have proposed a theistic biocentrism as the approach

---

37 Nash, *Loving Nature*, 107.

that most clearly reflects the biblical understanding. The eco-theology we espouse, however, evokes a number of possible responses and carries some obvious implications. Thus, I have proposed a revised, composite approach to stewardship. It is necessary now to examine the literature relating to a theology of mission to see how that might relate to ecological concern and theology.

It would be helpful if at the outset it were possible to establish an adequate and agreed definition of mission, but the difficulty of achieving that is reflected in the literature. More than that, in his classic work *Transforming Mission*, David Bosch cautions that mission is ultimately undefinable, and that we should never take it upon ourselves to "delineate mission too sharply and too self-confidently". The most we can hope for, Bosch argues, is "some *approximations* of what mission is all about"[38]. I contend that Bosch is essentially correct in his assessment that definitions are generally problematic, and that in large part an understanding of what mission is will emerge in the discussion.

In his public lecture entitled "The Third Mission of the Church", Norman Habel suggested that there have been three phases in the history of Christian mission, and this will be a useful structural tool in the discussion that follows.

Mission as "Saving Souls"

Habel's first mission of the Church represents an approach to mission that is largely confined to evangelism. In what may be regarded in some circles as a traditional approach to mission, and even more to the plural "missions", there is a strong focus on the human aspect, and some books on mission are almost totally human-focussed. But the issue involved is not only the human focus, but also and in particular that mission is perceived as little more than "the saving of souls" regardless of the circumstances in which people are living.

A typical example of the problem of definition is reflected by Dickson, who defines mission narrowly so that it becomes virtually synonymous with personal evangelism. Certainly it has a strong human focus: for him it is "the range of activities by which members of a religious community desirous of the conversion of outsiders seek to promote their religion to

---

38 Bosch, *Transforming*, 9.

non-adherents"[39]. But the problem of defining Christian mission as no more than a strategy for the conversion of people extends to a critical approach to other points of view.

Edward Schnabel takes the issue a little further in his *Early Christian Mission*, a massive 2-volume work of nearly 2,000 pages. In it he writes somewhat disparagingly of what he regards as some rather vague concepts of mission, as employed for example by the World Council of Churches, and which are used to include comprehensively all aims and activities of the Church, including care for creation, but (according to him) excluding "proselytism". Schnabel's view is obviously human-centred, and focussed on the communication of a message "to people of different faiths a new interpretation of reality" – of God, humanity, and salvation, and to win them over to this faith[40]. Clearly, any form of social or eco-justice is not on his radar.

In his *Mission of the New Testament*, Hahn appears to take the issue forward by referring to the kingdom of God, but the appearance is an illusion. Like Dickson and others, he explores mission in some of the major sectors of the New Testament, but again there is almost no recognition of mission beyond what might be termed evangelisation. But two points might be made. First, he states that "Matthew particularly points out the content of the gospel – it is a matter of preaching 'the gospel of the kingdom'"[41]. The question is, 'what is the gospel of the kingdom'? Hahn does not really help us. The implication appears to be that the task easily translates into missionary activity, or seeking converts to Christianity. Second, Hahn defines mission as "the Church's service, made possible by the coming of Christ and the eschatological event of salvation, and founded in Jesus' commission"[42]. But what does that mean? I contend that such a definition does not help us very much in understanding mission beyond the direct scope of evangelisation, as traditionally understood in individualistic or personal terms.

---

39 John P Dickson, 2003. *Mission-commitment in Ancient Judaism and in the Pauline Communities: the shape, extent and background of early Christian Mission.* (Tubingen: Mohr Siebeck, 2003), 10.

40 Eckhard J Schnabel, *Early Christian Mission.* (Downers Grove, Ill: InterVarsity Press; Leicester, Eng: Apollos, 2004), 11.

41 Ferdinand Hahn, *Mission in the New Testament.* (London: SCM Press, 1965), 122.

42 Hahn, *Mission*, 173.

Habel's charge is that the "first mission" people are guilty of an unsophisticated reading of "the Great Commission" of Matthew 28:19, the call to "make disciples of all nations." In many denominations, that translated into an emphasis on personal salvation and related issues. In practice, as Habel acknowledges, it meant more than that, in that the call of Jesus was to "make disciples", which is not quite the same as making converts, but nevertheless the emphasis was on "spiritual" dimensions, narrowly understood.

It is clear that evangelism is widely regarded as an essential element, indeed a priority, of a mission approach. However, there is also a popular perception that evangelism relates solely to a concern for individuals and their ultimate destiny, to "saving" what might be regarded as "disembodied souls". I have no argument with the proposition that evangelisation must be one of the priorities of Christian mission, that its task is to urge people to acknowledge Jesus Christ as Saviour and Lord, and thus to discover a personal faith in and relationship with God. My contention here is that it is more than that.

A strong human focus is reflected in a great many texts on mission; and even if a wider dimension is acknowledged, it is rarely extended in any practical sense. Furthermore, the majority of "how to" books focus almost exclusively on "winning people", or building up the Church. Having said that, it is important to add that no one is arguing against a human focus *per se*. Far from being a problem, the gospel is rightly understood as "good news" for people, and a significant part of the Church's work is inevitably bound up in "people issues". The problem resides, rather, in an *exclusively* human focus and the lack of attention to the prophetic element, in many cases, as I have suggested, to its total exclusion. The latter point at least is picked up in the "second mission".

Mission incorporating the Whole Human Being

Like the "first mission", the "second mission" is also human-centred; but for Habel it extends the personal "spiritual" focus "to include rescuing the whole human being as part of a community"[43], which is certainly an advance. Here the foundational text is Luke 4:18-19, or Jesus' synagogue sermon in which he quoted from Isaiah in order to express the kind of ministry he would

---

43 Habel, *Third Mission*, 32.

exercise. Thus, the spiritual implications are extended to the total human situation in all its physical, social, and even political aspects.

Loren Mead argues that the Church is living through a time of paradigm shift, and that it virtually needs to reinvent itself. There is a new mission frontier, and the old ways and structures will not be adequate. But certainly, Mead argues, Christians need to be turned outward towards the world. A "holy club" mentality that "responds to the mission frontier of the individual, but not of the community"[44] must be rejected. In a subsequent work Mead picks up the New Testament concept of *koinonia*, in which the Christian lives in a tension between his or her Church heritage and the public arena. Thus, Christians live within the tension of a number of polarities, and notably what Mead describes as "servanthood vs. conversion"[45]. The latter obviously relates to calling people into a faith relationship with God and the life of the Church; that is important, but it can become religious "scalp hunting". The former is based on the out-going servanthood of Jesus, but it can degenerate into sheer activism if it loses its depth and grounding. Mead concludes, "The local religious community of the future will have to move beyond the simplistic either/or we experience today. Servanthood vs conversion is not a choice to be made; it is a polarity that must be built into the structures we create for the Church"[46].

But the history of the Church in the last 100 years or so demonstrates that it is often not easy to embrace both the personal and social aspects of Christian mission. This is reflected in the work of Paul Avis. He defines mission as "the whole church bringing the whole Christ to the whole world", a definition he regards as holistic; certainly it includes "bringing prophetic critique to bear on unjust structures"[47]. At first that sounds more promising than the very human focus of previous definitions. Yet even here, it is clear that the primary focus is on the unchurched and the non-Christians. Avis acknowledges that non-human life is not "outside of God's care and our human response", yet because they are not "hearers and doers

---

44 Loren B Mead, *The Once and Future Church*. (Washington DC: The Alban Institute, 1991), 41.

45 Mead, *The Once and Future Church*, 46.

46 Mead, *The Once and Future Church*, 47.

47 Paul D L Avis, *A Ministry Shaped by Mission*. (London and New York: T & T Clark, 2005), 1.

of the word", they are by implication of lesser importance. He concludes, in my view somewhat simplistically, that "it is persons, created in the image of the personal God, who are on the receiving end of mission"[48].

A fundamental contradiction appears at the heart of Avis' approach. At one level he projects a wider concern, asserting that mission is the cutting edge of the church and cannot be reduced to evangelism. He cites Moltmann in terms of the goal of mission as being the consummation of all creation in God. But finally he comes back to the personal approach as the priority. However, an earlier book by Avis reflects much more clearly the broader aspects of mission. There he writes of "two mission agendas – the public, cultural, and social aspect … and the pastoral, local, and personal aspect", and adds that they "are not alternate strategies, but stand or fall together"[49]. Thus he asserts that the mission of the Church extends beyond the traditional pastoral mode. "The healing of the nations requires a mission that is carried forward on a broader front. Mission is not a discreet activity of the Church, but the cutting edge of the Church's life"[50].

Perhaps the struggle Avis appears to express in some of his work is similar to that of some of the twentieth century Evangelical Councils that tried, not altogether successfully, to balance the personal and social dimensions of mission. This is reflected in his reference to the final position of the International Missionary Council at Tambaran in 1938: "Tambaran by no means overlooks the missionary challenge of social transformation and the imperative to work for justice, freedom, and peace. But the dominant theme is the Church's calling 'so to exalt and proclaim' Jesus Christ that people are won to repentance, faith, and participation in the Church"[51].

Against such a background, it is appropriate to consider an approach to evangelism that relates well within that wider understanding of Christian mission, and it is one that is affirmed across a broad spectrum. It is expressed very clearly by the Australian evangelist, Alan Walker, who called for "a new, saner, larger evangelism" that will "draw together the personal and the social elements of the gospel, seeking at the same time the conversion of men

---

48 Avis, *A Ministry*, 4.
49 Paul D L Avis, *Church Drawing Near – Spirituality and Mission in a Post-Christian Culture.* (London: T & T Clark, 2003), 5.
50 Avis, *Church Drawing Near*, 13.
51 Avis, *A Ministry*, 18.

and women and the building of a society fit for people to live in"[52]. Walker exemplified that approach in practical terms as few others have done.

It should be noted that Walker is by no means alone in the stance he adopted during his life. A clear implication of the type of approach adopted by Walker and many others is that evangelism involved releasing the power of the gospel into the total context of the human situation. Thus, it involves more than simply winning individuals to the Christian way of life. If it is to be effective, then the conditions under which people live and to which they react, often with bitterness and even violence, must also feel the redeeming touch of the Church's life. In other words, it is not simply a matter of how many converts are needed in order to change the world; it is a question of how much the world must be changed in order to win converts.

From a Southern Baptist perspective in the United States, Findley Edge[53] made a similar point about the relationship between the personal and social dimensions of the Church's life and message, suggesting that both are essential elements of the one gospel, and we should give ourselves enthusiastically to both. He goes on to cite John Bright, who identifies that gospel as the gospel of the Kingdom of God, which of course includes a prophetic element

Thus, when evangelism is released from the shackles of an excessive individualism and is placed in the more holistic context of the New Testament, it becomes clear that mission and evangelism cease to be discreet entities, and tend to merge into one another. Nevertheless, such an understanding is in keeping with some broader definitions of mission encompassed by Habel's "second mission", and begins to relate to the emphasis Jesus placed on "the kingdom of God". Shenk and Kirk both pick up the wider implications of such a model.

Shenk defines mission as "the effort to effect the passage over the boundary between faith in Jesus Christ and its absence"[54], and goes on to indicate that it is prior to the Church and speaks of movement and purpose. When read at a superficial level it could be taken anthropocentrically. He writes

---

52 Alan Walker, *The New Evangelism*. (Belfast and Dublin: Christian Journals, 1977), 7.

53 Findley B Edge, *The Greening of the Church*. (Waco, Texas: Word Books, 1971).

54 Wilbert R Shenk, *Changing Frontiers of Mission*. (Maryknoll, New York: Orbis Books, 1999), xi.

of "God's redemptive mission"[55], a notion that is often assumed to have a human focus. However, Shenk goes on to emphasise the centrality of the reign of God as a mystery we don't fully grasp, and so a larger vision begins to emerge. For Shenk, the good news of the gospel is the good news of the kingdom of God, and "the animating centre of mission and of theology"[56]. Thus "mission is the means by which God's reign is being realized in the world"[57]. He points to five different ways in which the Bible understands "world", and one of those is as the object of God's mission. It is at this point that eco-mission becomes not only possible, but also indeed inevitable.

Kirk also picks up the theme of the kingdom of God, and suggests that it is only in such a context that the *missio Dei* can be understood[58]. Thus, for Kirk mission becomes the defining reality of the Church; "the Church ... intentionally bears witness to the meaning and relevance of the kingdom, while not itself being identical with that kingdom"[59]. The ecological implications of such a position are not lost on Kirk.

Mead takes this matter further, arguing that what is essential is *God's* mission, not the mission of the Church. Although it is clear that Christians and the Church have a role to play, he asserts that the mission of God is greater than that of the Church in its organizations. Thus Mead argues that God is at work in major movements outside the Church, including the environmental movement. "Current Church efforts to establish task forces on environmental issues may be worthwhile, but probably will have little impact. The task of the Church is to call people and send them into those places in which God's mission is already being done"[60]. That leads us directly to the third mission.

Holistic Mission: the Whole Earth

A vision of mission that is wider and deeper than a human-centred conversion approach becomes apparent in the affirmation that the Church

---

55 Shenk, *Changing Frontiers*, 9.
56 Shenk, *Changing Frontiers*, 10.
57 Shenk, *Changing Frontiers*, 15.
58 J Andrew Kirk, *What is Mission? Theological Explorations.* (London: Darton, Longman and Todd Ltd, 1999), 29.
59 Kirk, *What is Mission?* 36.
60 Loren B Mead, *Five Challenges for the Once and Future Church.* (Washington DC: The Alban Institute, 1996), 76.

is called to announce the reign of God, aiming for wholeness, inclusion, and service rather than domination. Thus, as the second mission included the concerns of the first mission, so the third mission of the Church for Habel moves beyond the earlier approaches to encompass the earth itself. "The task of this mission may be variously understood as saving, redeeming, restoring, liberating, or healing the earth[61]. The theme of reconciliation may also be relevant. It is not necessary here to debate the relative importance of the personal and social dimensions of mission; clearly both are important. Thus, eco-mission becomes part of a broader mission perspective.

Bevans and Schroeder make the point that while it is generally recognised that ecology, justice and peace belong together, "there has not been much reflection on how the preservation of the integrity of creation is linked to the church's mission. There is no question, however, that it is"[62]. It may be argued that such a position is changing; in any event, in a look forward to Christian mission of the 21st century, Bosch was prepared to be quite specific: "A missiology of Western culture must include an ecological dimension. The time is long past that we can afford to exclude the environment from our missionary agenda"[63].

But the process of moving forward with that agenda involves at least the identification of a number of negative images from past belief and practice. As Fowler and Habel both point out, this has much to do with some traditional theological expressions that in turn relate strongly to ancient dualisms, in which "spirit" is good and "matter" is evil. Thus, earth and heaven are compared and contrasted, to the definite disadvantage of the earth. Habel states that, as an example, in some Assemblies of God missions in the Kimberley region, there is strong opposition to land rights. "Your land rights are in heaven", is the cry; "Seeking land rights on earth is a temptation of the devil"[64]. When contrasted with the notion of a prosperity gospel, rife in some circles, such an approach may be viewed as an attempt to keep indigenous people in a depressed state.

---

61 Habel, *Third Mission*, 33.
62 Stephen B Bevans and Roger P Schroeder, *Constants in Context: A Theology of Mission for Today.* (Maryknoll, New York: Orbis Books, 2005), 375.
63 David J Bosch, *Believing in the Future: Towards a Missiology of Western Culture.* (Valley Forge, Penn.: Trinity Press International, 1995), 55.
64 Habel, *Third Mission*, 34.

A more common negative image may be that "the earth is temporal, transient and destined for disposal"[65], and thus the state of the earth is considered to be of little consequence. When faith's basic question is "where will you spend eternity?" the earth becomes no more than a staging post on the way to that more important goal. If, however, as this book asserts, it was God who created our earthly home and called it "good", then a new dimension is added to our understanding and mission.

In chapter 2 I attempted to indicate something of the scope of the crisis facing humankind and the earth, and that does not need to be restated here. However, three points made by Bosch and which are almost beyond dispute may serve to summarise the situation. First, the exploitation of the natural world and the resulting ecological damage began in the West. Second, the earth cannot survive if all peoples were to live in the manner of the Western countries; in other words, our lifestyle is not sustainable. And third, ecological exploitation in the developing world may be linked to a global economic structure that is determined by the West. Thus, it is appropriate to refer, as I did in chapter 2, to "the suffering of creation"; in view of the fact that people and their environment are clearly interdependent", and that humans have an enormous capacity to heal or to harm the earth and each other, eco-mission emerges as one of the essential aspects of a holistic mission response in these days.

On a more positive note, it may be helpful to recall that in recent decades the Church has been encouraged to understand "salvation" as extending beyond the human level to include the creation itself. Thus, with Habel, the gospel may be viewed as "good news" for the earth in three ways. These have largely been developed earlier in this book, but may be mentioned briefly. First, God has not abandoned the earth, and the divine covenant with the earth remains. Second, God suffers with the earth. Duchrow and Liedke[66] also pick up this theme; for them, the suffering of God is seen in the cross of Jesus. Habel makes the connection with the earth strongly:

> Do you want to see Christ suffering? ... First look at the cross. Then look at hundreds of stations of the cross scattered around the earth. At every station God suffers. To name just a few: Maralinga in Australia, Ok Tedi in Papua New Guinea, the Amazon Rain Forest, the saline farmlands of

---

65 Habel, *Third Mission*, 35.
66 Duchrow and Liedke, *Shalom*.

Western Australia, the Gulag of Siberia, or the lost soil from the Darling Downs. God en-soiled in this desecrated earth suffers[67].

But third, God's suffering with humanity extended beyond the cross; "God was in Christ, reconciling the world (cosmos) to himself" (2nd Cor. 5:19a). Life therefore rises out of death, as "with this rainbow covenant (Gen. 9:10) God began the long way of salvation for the cosmos, which reached its decisive stage with the reconciliation of the world in the cross of Jesus"[68]. Thus, as Bevans and Schroeder put it, spiritual wholeness through the gospel "reflects the love of a God who expresses the divine identity in total solidarity with creation"[69].

As a practical expression of such an approach, one of the more significant mission statements of recent times has been the Anglican document known as *MISSIO 2000*[70]. In line with authors cited above, the document asserts that while the Church is marked by the sins of humankind, it similarly reflects its solidarity with the suffering of the world, and it is at just this point that it is possible to see the emergence of an eco-mission theology. In the years 1984 to 1990 the Anglican Consultative Council formulated "Five Marks of Mission" – a list of quite specific basic principles of mission – which the Report[71] notes have won "wide acceptance" among Anglicans around the world:

- To proclaim the good news of the kingdom of God.
- To teach, baptise, and nurture new believers.
- To respond to human need by loving service.
- To seek to transform the unjust structures of society.
- To strive to safeguard the integrity of creation, and sustain and renew the life of the earth.

Thus, what was previously implicit was now made quite explicit, especially in the fourth and fifth points. The first three points might suggest a traditional approach to mission, and there is no problem with that. Likewise

---

67 Habel, *Third Mission*, 40.
68 Duchrow and Liedke, *Shalom*, 53.
69 Bevans and Schroeder, *Constants*, 377.
70 Eleanor Johnson and John Clark, eds. *Anglicans in Mission: a Transforming Journey*. (London: SPCK, 2000).
71 Johnson and Clark, *Anglicans*, 19-20.

the transformation of unjust structures in society is not new. It is the final point that is of particular interest in that it clearly identifies the basis of a valid eco-mission. The Report includes a definition of mission adapted from a Statement of the Commission for Mission of the National Council of Churches in Australia (NCCA):

> Mission is the creating, reconciling and transforming action of God, flowing from the community of love found in the Trinity, made known to all humanity in the person of Jesus, and entrusted to the faithful action and witness of the people of God who, in the power of the Spirit, are a sign, foretaste, and instrument of the reign of God[72]

The "Five Marks" were subsequently revisited for the sake of clarification and elaboration. Thus the various facets of the mission of the Church, which is the mission of Christ, and includes eco-mission, may be seen as an expression of the proclamation of the good news of the kingdom of God. More than that, it is contextual, is expressed as celebration and thanksgiving, and as God-in-action as this mission goes out from God.

Mead asserts, correctly I believe, that the primary mission is God's, and that the role of the Church is not to try to control mission but to celebrate it, to participate in it, and to bring a faith heritage to bear on issues such as the eco-crisis. But his downbeat assessment of Church-based ecological groups would be hotly disputed by significant groups such as Au Sable in the USA or EcoCongregation in Britain. As an organization based in Britain, EcoCongregation is very active in encouraging local congregations to develop a significant environmental mission agenda, and the role of such organizations will be developed in some depth in a subsequent chapter.

But while the Church does not necessarily need to establish its own parallel structures to replicate what secular organizations are already doing effectively, it is nevertheless essential for a specifically Christian voice to be heard within that wider forum. Even if a secular humanist may not necessarily be convinced of that need, there are nevertheless still several reasons why that should be so. I contend that it is important for the Church itself, for the integrity of the gospel it proclaims, and for the environmental contribution it is able to make alongside other people of goodwill, even if some are not people of faith. Any perception in environmental circles

---

72 Johnson and Clark, *Anglicans*, 21.

or the wider community that Christianity has nothing positive to say in the eco-crisis needs to be challenged. Christians themselves need to be educated, and to that end some structural organization may be required to facilitate participation.

Postmodern Context

There are several crucial areas of contextuality, and in terms of eco-mission several aspects may be identified. At a fundamental level, eco-mission must take account of the fact that Western society is overwhelmingly postmodern in orientation, and that brings with it both challenge and opportunity. Three aspects in particular offer a real point of connection between the eco-aware Church and the population at large.

The first of these is the increasing environmental awareness and concern in the community, focussed for example in issues of climate change, global warming, or even the price of fuel. Until relatively recent times, many have believed that the Church has nothing meaningful to say on this subject. Anecdotal evidence suggests that this has tended to be the perception of many in the environmental movement, and that has not been helped by the nature-denying strand of Christian thinking, the ambiguity to which Santmire referred, or the charge that Christianity and dominion theory is largely to blame for the crisis. Against such a background, an ecologically-aware Christian community could make a significant mission impact.

Second, there is a re-sacralising of nature that often expresses itself in environmentalism or even a revived paganism. The sacred element in nature has been recovered, but at the cost of a distinction between God and nature. If the Church can recover the immanent side of a panentheistic God and present such a message, there is a possibility of connecting with people at that level. The emphasis here is on the word "possibility"; there can be no guarantee that a secularist ecologist will be convinced, but the notion of immanence at least increases the possibility of people grasping a legitimate Christian position.

A third aspect, rising out of the second, may be the importance of relationships for the postmodern generation. It follows therefore that a presentation of the Christian message in relational terms may be both authentic and productive. If people tend to see relationship as much more important than dogma, it may be that they will also see their relationships with other life and nature generally as important, and that this will therefore provide an important point of connection for Christian mission. This of course raises much wider issues, but it is nonetheless consistent with an eco-mission approach.

Postmodernism also presents a real problem. As Bosch states, "It is a permissive society, without norms, models, and traditions, an immediate society, without past and often without future"[73]; consequently many people live on the basis that they will see about tomorrow if and when it arrives. In addition to that, there is a vast amount of new information and an increasing multiplicity of choices and challenges leading to a breakdown of established worldviews and a loss of certainty in many cases. But there are many aspects involved here, including ways in which both harmful and helpful new information may be accessed, an array of new technologies and ways of communicating, the confusion between reality and virtual reality, not to mention substance abuse and resultant crime problems or HIV-AIDS. Bosch is not alone in perceiving the gap between vision and reality as something that presents a crisis in worldview for individuals and communities alike. It is not difficult to see how this worldview crisis might shape an approach to the future in ways that are almost impossible to predict, not least in terms of eco-mission.

But there is another quite different sense in which context is important. The ultimate context in which Christian eco-mission is set is of course global. It is increasingly apparent that the global biosphere knows nothing about national or even continental boundaries, and that whatever we do, or fail to do, has global implications. However, there is also a more immediate context in which eco-mission is exercised and to which it must relate. Thus, an eco-mission group in the Daintree rainforest area of North Queensland would have a rather different local agenda from a group in the vast Murray-Darling basin, or even the Sunshine Coast tourist strip of Queensland. A locally identified agenda within an overall global framework will provide the best possibility of relevance and effectiveness.

---

73 Bosch, *Believing*, 3.

Conclusion

It may be observed that for much of the Church's history the theological consensus has been at best ambivalent about ecological matters, an ambiguity that was clearly identified by Paul Santmire. However, as I identified in the previous chapter, in recent decades the balance has shifted, and an enormous volume of ecotheological literature has emerged. In the Church at large the problem has been that there has tended to be a disconnection between theory and praxis. A central argument of this book is that in terms of a practical theology, those two components need to be brought together.

A further observation may be that with some notable exceptions, a great deal of the theology of Christian mission has been human oriented. More than that, many of the more popular "how to" books and articles in recent decades have focussed largely on how to "win people" or grow larger churches. In many cases, the wider dimension that is identified is still human focussed, in terms of Habel's "second mission" of the Church.

I have argued that biblical theology requires an ecotheology in terms of what I have described as "theistic biocentrism". From that standpoint I have drawn out a number of implications or responses that are required, in terms of the "third mission" of the Church that encompasses the Earth as a whole. Thus I have argued for a composite model based on a revised notion of stewardship.

A theology of ecological mission will therefore have its roots in ecotheology, in the biblical mandate for mission rather than in pragmatism. In a primary sense this will be expressed globally, in general principles that will hold firm regardless of any particular circumstances. But a theology of eco-mission will ultimately need to be worked through and expressed in a myriad of different and particular situations by local congregations.

CHAPTER SIX

The Big Picture

In previous chapters we have considered some of the ways in which care of the natural environment, God's creation, is expressed in theology, and how that is then carried over into our understanding of Christian mission. But when we think about the Church, many of us would have to admit that we think primarily of our own denomination, or even more narrowly, of the congregation of which we may be part. On the other hand, if we think of that iconic picture of a fragile planet Earth hanging in space, a rather different focus comes to mind as we realise that this is our home.

That image of Earth from space is an invitation to consider what we might call "the big picture", not only in terms of the way in which ecumenical, confessional and denominational groups have responded, but also of the interfaith and wider community dimensions. It is true that the Christian community has a particular and unique contribution to offer in the care of God's creation, but we cannot do this alone. At the end of the day this is a whole of humanity issue, and as Earth beings first of all it is important to see how this fits together on the larger screen.

An Interfaith Approach

In his book *The Church and Climate Change*, Ernst Conradie indicates the need for a broad approach: "Remarkably, Christians will only be able to hear God's word in conversation with people from other living faiths at the dialogue table – since climate change, perhaps for the first time in human history, is a challenge that can only be addressed through a collective, indeed a global effort[1]".

If the potential is significant in Christian terms, it may be even greater when viewed in interfaith terms. The fact is that in terms of the care of the natural environment there is substantial agreement across virtually all world faiths, and there could be few better ways of breaking down barriers than sharing in the care of the only home we all have – the Earth itself. Some decades ago when I was heavily involved in the ecumenical movement, it was common

---

1 Ernst Conradie. *The Church and Climate Change*. (Pietermaritzburg, South Africa: Cluster Publications, 2008), 101.

for the Greek word *oikoumene*, on which the word "ecumenical" is based, to be defined as relating to the whole inhabited world. In common usage it tends to have a far more restricted meaning, but that original meaning was important in that it was always a challenge to expand our horizon. That challenge is still apt, especially in today's world when our perspective is often so limited.

I want to suggest that there are a number of factors that offer a powerful incentive to explore a more ambitious goal. The first is that in many of the world's religions today, including Christianity, there is a minority who hold what could only be described as extreme and intolerant positions with the effect of driving deep divisions between people, groups, nations, and often within nations. The painful and often dangerous outcome of this development is all too obvious.

The second factor is also a global one in every sense, and that is the pain of planet Earth. Again, it is not my purpose here to elaborate on that point; as I have suggested, the effects of climate change and non-sustainable ways of living are increasingly obvious, but inevitably they have their greatest impact on the poorest people who have had little input into the cause of the problem and who are least able to respond to it. But more than that, non-human life also has intrinsic value with its inclusion in the Rainbow Covenant of Genesis 9, and has no response capacity at all. But we are all in this together as part of what has been called "the web of life", and we, together with all life, are bound to suffer with a groaning Earth.

The third factor is crucial. Just as Christian environmental Statements express fundamental agreement across virtually all confessional positions and divisions, so there is broad agreement among world faiths. As an example of that agreement the United Nations Environment Programme (UNEP) established the Interfaith Partnership for the Environment as a project in 1986; in 2000 the Partnership published a book called *Earth and Faith: A Book of Reflection for Action*. As the Director of the UNEP explained, this was the result of an effort "to continue the dialogue between the scientific and faith communities" from which, it is hoped, will emerge "a greater commitment to taking responsible actions for the protection of our environment for our common good."[2]

---

2 Libby Bassett, ed. 2000. *Earth and Faith: a book of reflection for action.* New York: The United Nations Environment Programme.

There are two issues in that. The first is a positive partnership between faith and science, especially in the area of ecological issues and challenges. In brief, the interface of faith and science that we dealt with in Chapter 2 represents an important and fruitful partnership. Through ecologists and others, science has been playing a truly prophetic role for a number of years now. It has alerted us to what we are doing to the environment, and what the consequences will be if we keep living in an unsustainable way. Faith and spirituality for its part touches deeper levels of purpose and belonging. We clearly need the contribution of both.

The second issue rising out of the UN book is the way in which the major world faiths converge in their attitude to environmental care, in spite of the differences between world faiths in other areas or the environmental negatives that have emanated from religious sources from time to time. Authorised representatives from the Muslim, Buddhist, Jewish, Hindu, Christian and other faiths each wrote a short first-hand account of their Faith's teaching on environmental care, and the result is striking; in real terms they are in remarkable agreement on this issue, as they all enjoin their followers to a response of care.

The clear outcome of this convergence of belief is that the care of the planet may be a rich area not only for fruitful interfaith dialogue but also for common action. The Director of the UNEP Adrian Amin wrote that "We … view the convergence of spiritual values and their respect for the environment as an inspiration for environmental actions today so that our succeeding generations may all be beneficiaries of a healthy planet and a development that is sustainable"[3]. It is not difficult to find some recent examples of the kind of collaboration I am advocating.

First, in the last several years we have witnessed the formation of a new national body known as the ARRCC, or Australian Religious Response to Climate Change, which has given practical expression to the UNEP's hope. This is described as "a multi-faith network taking action on the most pressing issue of our time." The website affirms that "In the face of ecological damage and social injustices, we affirm our love for this planet and its inhabitants and our deep reverence for life.[4]"

---

3 *Earth and Faith*, p4.
4 www.arrcc.org.au

Second, in 2010, the International Year for Biodiversity, I was personally involved as part of an interfaith panel for World Environment Day at the University of the Sunshine Coast in Queensland; an Islamic scholar, a Jewish Rabbi, and a Buddhist Environmental Educator, together with a trained moderator completed the panel. As the panel members discussed the topic, with each reflecting on it from their own faith perspective, the high level of agreement was obvious to everyone in the auditorium. I believe that made a profound impression.

Third, another event in 2010 was at Southern Cross Care, a Catholic Aged Care Facility at Caloundra, where a public service was held to pray for peace and reconciliation. At least two things stood out for me. The first was the obvious point that many of the people attending were aged, but no less committed to the ideal for all that. The second was that speakers from the Muslim, Jewish, Buddhist, and Christian traditions all spoke, and as was the case at the University of the Sunshine Coast, although coming out of differing traditions, they all said essentially the same thing. The spirit of goodwill and the desire for peace and reconciliation was heart-warming.

The fourth experience was a public lecture on "Islam, Justice, and Compassion" by Imam Afroz Ali at the University of Queensland in October 2009. Afroz Ali is Founder and president of the Al-Ghazzali Centre for Islamic Sciences and Human Development which runs Muslim and interfaith educational, philanthropic, social justice and environmental programs in Sydney and Samoa. He advocates peace, acceptance, justice and inter-personal rights and is involved in the international organisation, "Charter for Compassion". His lecture focussed primarily on the Centre's environmental work in Sydney, and included slides of the work being carried out by groups of people. My Christian spirit resonated with his approach, and led to a hope that it is a work we could share.

Sometimes our spiritual and religious outlook is too restricted. Sometimes our world view is too limited. Sometimes an innate suspicion of anyone who is "different" from us obscures a more fruitful way forward. The Earth – our home – is in need of a mission dedicated to its wellbeing, and it is precisely that need which presents us not only with a profound challenge, but also with a great opportunity to see each other, and the faith traditions we represent, in a new light. There could surely be no better way to break down barriers and build bridges than to focus on the bigger picture of the planet. Moreover, the UN book suggests that:

> *The spiritual challenge of the ecological crisis draws us back to our religious traditions, to reflect on and celebrate the natural world in its most profound sense of mystery as a manifestation and experience of the sacred.*[5]

International and Ecumenical Responses

In more specific Christian terms, Statements have been made and actions determined at the broadest level of national and international affairs, and while these may not impact greatly on actions at a local level, they do form an essential context in which further action is possible. In that regard, it is worthy of note that commitment to an ecological mission agenda covers a wide spectrum of what might be called the religious community. Several examples of significant agreement could be cited.

The World Council of Churches (WCC) has had a significant role through its unit, Justice, Peace and the Integrity of Creation, and has contributed to the debate through a range of books and publications. But one example may serve to highlight both the possibilities and limitations of action at this level. The WCC participated in the Earth Summit at Rio de Janeiro in 1992, and later in that year published *Redeeming the Creation*. Clearly the book contains useful reflections on the Summit and other valuable insights, including a Letter to the Churches. Council delegates wrote, as they said, "with a sense of urgency". Their words are stark: "The earth is in peril. Our only home is in plain jeopardy. We are at the precipice of self-destruction. For the very first time in the history of creation, certain life support systems of the planet are being destroyed by human actions"[6]. Later in the letter they stated, "You will understand why our hearts are heavy and why it is extremely urgent that we as churches make strong and permanent spiritual, moral and material commitments to the emergence of new models of society, based in deepest gratitude to God for the gift of life and in respect for the whole of God's creation"[7].

The impact of such a considered and impassioned plea should have reverberated around churches all over the world, but it is doubtful if many

---

5 *Earth and Faith*, p7.
6 Granberg-Michaelson, *Redeeming*, 70.
7 Granberg-Michaelson, *Redeeming*, 71.

even knew of the Letter's existence, and still less, read it and acted upon it. But a similar call to action from within the same ecumenical family came from the United States, where the National Council of Churches convened a conference in 2005. This resulted in an Open Letter to Church and Society in the United States, entitled *God's Earth is Sacred*. Again, it is a considered Statement, and contains crucial insights relating to ecological theology and mission. The "Call to Action" is based on a strong foundation that I would contend has implications for eco-mission in and through the Church generally. It begins with the confession that for too long Christians have pushed the care of the Earth to the periphery of their agenda. It continues:

> This is *not* a competing 'program alternative', one 'issue' among many. In this most critical moment in Earth's history, we are convinced that *the central moral imperative* of our time is care for Earth as God's creation.... We believe that caring for creation must undergird, and be entwined with, all other dimensions of our churches' ministries. We are convinced that it is no longer acceptable to claim to be 'church' while continuing to perpetuate, or even permit, the abuse of Earth as God's creation"[8].

It is noteworthy that the Statement was signed by some of the most prominent eco-theologians of recent times, including Nash, Rasmussen, Santmire, Cobb, McFague, and others. Thus, while it is directed to American Christians, its significance is in reality universal, and could well be one of the foundational pillars of regional and local eco-mission. However, this raises a dilemma and a frustration that many jurisdictions experience, in that it is almost impossible to gauge the impact of official statements and resolutions of international or even national bodies, however strong and well-written they may be.

An "Evangelical Declaration on the Care of Creation"[9] was formulated in 1994 by the Evangelical Environmental Network in the United States, and while it reflects a different theological orientation, its content is broadly similar to other such statements. This Declaration acknowledges the degradation of creation, and lists land degradation, deforestation, species extinction, water degradation, global toxification, the alteration of atmosphere, and human and cultural degradation as particular issues. It

---

8 U.S. National Council of Churches. 2005. "God's Earth is Sacred". www.ncccusa.org. Retrieved February 2006.
9 Berry, *Care*, 18.

then sets out four spiritual responses involving both attitudes and actions. "The earthly result of human sin," it declares, "has been a perverted stewardship, a patchwork of garden and wasteland in which the waste is increasing…"[10]. The call to action includes the following: "We call upon Christians to listen to and work with all those who are concerned about the healing of creation, with an eagerness both to learn from them and also to share with them our conviction that the God whom all people sense in creation (Acts 17:27) is known fully only in the Word made flesh in Christ the living God who made and sustains all things"[11].

There have been a number of significant Roman Catholic Statements over recent decades. For example, in "Sollicitudo Rei Socialis" in 1987 Pope John Paul 11 wrote:

> The first consideration is the appropriateness of acquiring a growing awareness of the fact that one cannot use with impunity the different categories of beings, whether living or inanimate – animals, plants, the natural elements – simply as one wishes, according to one's own economic needs. On the contrary, one must take into account the nature of each being and of its mutual connection in an ordered system, which is precisely the cosmos[12].

A comprehensive document "Building a new Culture: Central Themes in Recent Church Teaching on the Environment" has emerged from the Episcopal Commission for Justice and Peace of the Canadian Province of Catholic Bishops"[13]. It concludes with the prayer "May the Lord grant to Catholics and to all people of good will the virtue of hope, so that we will not lose heart as we strive to safeguard our environment". Other Roman Catholic Statements include John Paul 11's call in 2001 for "ecological conversion", a Joint Declaration with Ecumenical Patriarch Bartholomew 1 in 2002, and declarations from Pope Benedict XV1. More recently, at his installation Mass in March 2013 Pope Francis said "Let us be 'protectors' of creation, **protectors of God's plan inscribed in nature, protectors of one another and of the environment. Let us not allow omens of destruction and death to accompany the advance of this world!"**

---

10 Berry, *Care*, 18.
11 Berry, *Care*, 21-22.
12 Cited in Denis Edwards, *Jesus and the Natural World*, (Mulgrave, Vic: Garratt, 2012), 72.
13 Episcopal Commission for Justice and Peace of the Canadian Province of Catholic Bishops. *Building a new Culture: Central Themes in Recent Church Teaching on the Environment.* Jan 2013

There are other such documents and websites of course, such as the strong Statement by the Canada and Bermuda Division of The Salvation Army or the American-based Lutheran Earthkeeping Network of the Synods (LENS), and while some may want to change the occasional word, phrase, or even emphasis, the most significant point to emerge is the degree of unanimity from across the theological spectrum. As I have argued in previous chapters, the need to care for creation is acknowledged by Catholics, Orthodox, Evangelicals, Ecumenists, mainline Protestants and others. Such a consensus at a world level provides a significant backdrop for national declarations in Australia. An important addition here is that LENS provides both resources and encouragement for local congregations to become involved in eco-mission.

In 2006 the National Council of Churches in Australia issued a statement entitled "Sustaining Creation" that was addressed to the governments in Australia. This raised a number of basic issues that need not be revisited here, but it noted that while they were political and economic issues, they were moral and spiritual in nature. The strength of the Statement is in its recognition of the importance of environmental issues; its weakness lies in the fact that while it acknowledges that "we will do all in our power through the Churches" to act in ways that will assist in the achievement of its listed environmental goals, it is primarily a Statement about what governments should do.

There is only one conclusion we can draw from this brief overview, and that is that while there may be some small variations in emphasis, the Christian Church in general is of one mind about our need to be responsible carers of the natural environment which is God's creation. But there is an ever-present danger that such policy statements, generated with the best of intention, will have little effect. A much greater intentionality is imperative if their potential and purpose is to be realised.

The Role of Denominational Hierarchies

The role of denominational hierarchies can be important from both a positive and a negative point of view. It is reasonable, I believe, to suggest that in general the Church's role has been mixed. Some probably valid criticism has indicated that denominations have tended to act on their own rather than support existing cross-denominational programs. On the other hand, there are some significant initiatives, some of which are unambiguously positive, and that may be illustrated initially by reference to the British scene.

First, several years ago the Church of England was able to boast that it had an Environmental Advisor in every Diocese in England, and some of them are highly qualified in that field; and if, as appears to be the case, local congregations do not always feel supported by the denomination, it should be pointed out that the Advisors are invariably operating on a very part time basis.

Second, many Dioceses in England have held an educational eco day as part of the denomination's environmental effort. I had the opportunity to attend one such event for the Kensington Diocesan area in London; several hundred people were in attendance for the day, many of them clergy, and the line-up of speakers was very good. It would have provided plenty of "food for thought" for those who had previously not had much exposure to eco-theological and mission issues. Ironically, however, tea and coffee was served in disposable polystyrene cups!

Third, "Shrinking the Footprint" is another significant program of the Church of England. The stated aim of this program's first challenge is "to make a difference in the future through a growing series of strategic initiatives and partnerships which will change Church activities, structures, and processes, producing sustainable reductions in the Church of England's carbon emissions to 40% of current levels by 2050 – 'the 40% Church'.[14]" Moreover, the Shrinking the Footprint Path sets out some simple steps to make a difference.

A fourth area is the development of an environmental policy, as formulated, for example, by the Diocese of Ripon and Leeds. This affirms its commitment to the 5th Mark of Mission to which I referred in chapter 5, and which calls the Church "to strive to safeguard the integrity of creation and sustain and renew the earth." The Policy itself is comprehensive, and covers awareness, energy, water, waste, travel, materials and resources, as well as buildings and the natural environment. It goes on to address implementation, monitoring, and review, and includes a summary of useful resources.

---

14 (www.shrinkingthefootprint.cofe.anglican.org)

At the time of my visit to the UK the Roman Catholic Church did not appear to have a significant eco-mission infrastructure in place, although some leading individuals were working to change that. The Methodist Church is of course a much smaller denomination, but is nevertheless relatively active environmentally. It claims that in the year 2000 it became the first denomination to produce an Environmental Policy, a document that covered theology briefly and practical implications more extensively. The Church's principal environmental advocate claimed that the Methodist Church was the first to switch its headquarters to green electricity, and together with the United Reformed Church was the primary source of funding for EcoCongregation.

In Australia also an unequivocal response appears to have come from the major Churches. One of the key responses from the Roman Catholic Church is through Catholic Earthcare, which was formed by the Australian Catholic Bishops' Conference in 2002. Its role is to act as an advisory agency to the Bishops' Commission for Justice, Ecology and Development (BCJED) on ecological matters, including the safeguarding of the integrity of creation, environmental justice and ecological sustainability. Among other things it is called to stimulate and sustain the ecological conversion and prepare an environment for future generations that is closer to the plan of the Creator[15].

I made reference in chapter 5 to the Anglican Church's "5th Mark of Mission", "to strive to safeguard the integrity of creation, and sustain and renew the life of the earth", and that clearly informs the approach of that Church at a national level. A Report entitled "Green by Grace"[16] was prepared for the 2004 General Synod, and consciously built on the Anglican Communion's "Five Marks of Mission". This short but thoughtful paper includes the following: "Recognising that God sustains and saves all creation, and appoints people as stewards, we can honour God only if we act with care and respect not only for other people but for all the earth". However, the list of "practical responses" is somewhat less comprehensive.

The Australian Anglican Environmental Network website states hopefully, and I believe correctly, that "increasingly the Church is embracing the care

---

15 www.catholicearthcare.org.au accessed 18th August 2013.
16 Anglican General Synod. *Green by Grace*. Report. 2004.

of the environment and creation as an essential part of Christian faith, mission and outreach." Such a claim is given substance by the "Protection of the Environment Canon 2007" passed by the General Synod in October 2007. In brief, the Canon aims at reducing the environmental footprint of a Diocese and increasing environmental sustainability, giving leadership in care of the environment, as well as undertaking an educative role in the responsible care of God's creation. Importantly, once individual dioceses have adopted the Canon, they are thereby committed to report to the General Synod on targets and progress.

At its inaugural national Assembly in June 1977, the Uniting Church in Australia declared that "we are concerned with the basic human rights of future generations and will urge the wise use of energy, the protection of the environment and the replenishment of the earth's resources for their use and enjoyment." While the precise wording of that resolution may require updating, it does at least reflect an on-going commitment to the care of creation. Indeed, an environmental concern is enshrined in the Basis of Union itself.

Moreover, the sixth Assembly in 1991 passed what amounts to a Bill of Rights – namely, "The Rights of Nature and the Rights of Future Generations". This is a significant document that is set within the context of the divine covenant. It affirms "the inalienable dignity of all humans", and therefore calls for a guarantee of human rights, but extends that to a responsibility for future generations as well as for nature as God's creation. "We call upon the churches to make room for God's covenant with creation within the realm of law by committing themselves at all levels to recognition of the following 'Rights of Future Generations' and 'Rights of Nature'"[17].

The 2006 Assembly adopted a statement entitled "For the Sake of the Planet and all its People" relating to climate change. In brief, this was a call for Church members and congregations to minimise greenhouse emissions and to advocate for governments "to implement policies that significantly reduce our dependence on fossil fuels and increase our use of non-nuclear renewable energy sources." The paper itself covers a range of material that has already been canvassed; however, the cornerstone of its approach is arguably the following affirmation: "The Uniting Church's

---

17 Sixth Assembly of the Uniting Church in Australia, 1991.

commitment to the environment arises out of the Christian belief that God, as the Creator of the universe, calls us into a special relationship with the creation – a relationship of mutuality and interdependence which seeks the reconciliation of all creation with God"[18].

More than that, the Uniting Church has never been shy about engagement with the political processes in pursuit of what it believes. Thus, as part of the preparation for the last three Federal elections the Church issued guidelines and key issues for Church members and others to consider in determining how they should vote. Not surprisingly, that included issues related to the environment.

There is a danger that at a hierarchical level, organisational arrangements could lead to a separation of eco-mission and what may be considered more "mainstream" mission. I do not propose to analyse this issue here, but the question remains as to where eco-mission fits within Church structures. There is no one single way in which this can be handled, but my concern about the separation of eco-mission and mission remains. Theologically they belong together as an expression of the divine charter for God's people, and practically a separation runs a very great risk of a downgrading of ecological mission to a secondary role at best. Further, if eco-mission is truly regarded as part of the mainstream of what the Church is about then it is critical that it has a place in the budgets of the Churches.

State-level and Regional Responses

It is clear that at a national level, the Anglican, Uniting, and Roman Catholic Churches have for the most part expressed an unambiguous commitment to care of the environment as God's creation. In some cases, environmental resolutions pre-dated current popular perceptions by a large margin. Such affirmations at a national level form a solid foundation for other levels of the Church in this area of concern, but the determination of practical action is generally made at a more regional level.

Within the Anglican Church of Australia, a number of Dioceses have a Commission for the Environment broadly in order to encourage eco-mission within its boundaries. Several examples may serve to illustrate what is being done at this level. One leader in the field has been the Canberra-Goulburn Diocese. Its Commission reflects a wide diversity of skills and

---

18 Eleventh Assembly, Uniting Church in Australia, 2006.

life experience, and aims to encourage the care of creation both within the Church and in the wider community; to that end it seeks to support people in the Diocese, to provide information, and to act in an advocacy role. The work of the Commission is divided into sub-programs covering such things as liturgy, facilitation of group discussions, energy, education, environmental audits, water, and public advocacy. Its website provides links to significant other groups in the UK, the US, Canada and South Africa.

The Grafton Diocese in New South Wales has also been very active in this area. One initiative has been the production of a booklet called *Building a Better Relationship with our World: A Green Guide for People in Parishes.* Another initiative is the Riverbank Rainforest Restoration Project, relating to the Clarence River upstream from Susan Island, with implications for Aboriginal people and for biodiversity. This project was originally established by the 1st International Philosophy, Science and Theology Festival, with the aim of focussing on the whole of life rather than on the individual parts; members of the Grafton Ngerri Local Aboriginal Land Council, representing the traditional owners, cooperate in the Project. Other projects relate to Fairtrade, and the placement of photovoltaic cells on the roof of the General Manager's house as a way to showcase environmental actions in an average home.

A third example is the Diocese of Brisbane environmental group called AngliGreen, which offers a good and effective model of positive action in which both Church members and clergy, currently about 30 in all, can be drawn together from various Parishes for support and shared action. Through a spokesperson, Miriam Nyrene, the group stated, "We felt strongly that we needed to have a body at diocesan level to promote the need for all Christians to care for God's Creation and to try to halt and, if possible, heal some of the damage that we humans have done to the earth over many years. We aim to make ourselves available to help parishes with sustainability and practical initiatives they might wish to engage in"[19]. AngliGreen has a concise Vision Statement and clear Mission Goals, and is demonstrably reaching into what might be termed the "grassroots" of Church and community life.

---

19 Personal communication, 2008.

One of the strong ways in which the Roman Catholic Church has responded is through Catholic Education. In Queensland they established a Task Group in 2008 which developed a position statement on ecological sustainability titled "Creation...we care". The purpose of the Statement was to serve as a reminder that as Christians we have a call to care for creation for present and future generations. The Task Group declared that "we in Brisbane Catholic Education recognize and affirm that care for the environment is a sacred duty. Our commitment to our children and our children's children calls us to engage with our stewardship of creation through thought, words and actions". "Creation...we care" reflects the writings of Pope John Paul 11, who on 17 January 2001, called on the world's Catholics to make a commitment to avoid ecological "catastrophe". Pope Benedict XVI also wrote that, "God's creation is one and it is good. The concerns for non-violence, sustainable development, justice and peace, and care for our environment are of vital importance for humanity"[20].

The Queensland Synod is typical of Uniting Church Synods throughout Australia; it has passed a series of environmental resolutions over a period of years starting in 1989, many of which were relatively inconsequential, although the potential they contained did not always seem to materialise. But resolutions of the 2007 Synod were more substantial and covered a number of aspects. At one level it called on congregations and Church members to conduct an energy audit with a view to reducing greenhouse gas emissions, and to change to "Green Power". But the Synod went further than that. It determined that a Working Group should be set up, to include all significant groups and commissions related to the Synod, in order to "collate and promote the work currently being done to reduce the production of greenhouse gas emissions, to explore ways of further reducing those emissions, and to report progress to the Council of Synod within 6 months. Moreover, action was to be taken in three other ways; an environmental audit was to be conducted on the Uniting Church Centre, training on climate change, energy auditing and efficiency was to be provided, and a report on recommended future action was to go to the following Synod. Given that it is not easy to determine meaningful action at this level, these resolutions and the reporting mechanism put in place suggest a Church that is serious about trying to deal with environmental issues.

---

20 esd.bne.catholic.edu.au accessed 18th Aug 2013

There is much more that could and even should be said, but the purpose of this brief survey has been illustrative rather than comprehensive, and clearly it is a picture that is constantly changing.

Ecumenical Groups

Some ecumenical environmental groups have begun to emerge in the Australian context, and I will refer in particular to the NCCA Eco-Mission Project which was formed in March 2011. The rational behind the formation of this body was expressed thus:

> Given the current environmental crisis and a broad ecumenical consensus surrounding it, there is an urgent need for the churches to address publicly the ethical, social and spiritual questions posed by the crisis. There is also a growing awareness that the church has a mission to love and care for creation as a vital expression of its faith. It is therefore timely to establish a group that might facilitate this mission.

The Eco-Mission Project's Terms of Reference were:

1. Network with the relevant church bodies to enable the resources relating to care of creation to be shared.

2. Raise ecological consciousness and clarify the importance of facing the current environmental crisis as vital to the role of the church in society.

3. Foster an education in eco-mission that is grounded in our common biblical, theological, ecological and ethical traditions and animates participating churches to pursue their eco-mission.

4. Promote eco-mission as an integral part of the mission of the church and work towards an ecumenical consensus around this area of the church's mission.

5. Encourage church bodies and congregations to become public advocates against practices that pollute, degrade or destroy domains of God's creation.

6. Explore best practice models for the sustainability of God's creation that would be appropriate for local churches to adopt.

7. Contribute to national events and create resources that will publicise, promote and help facilitate a program of ecological mission among the church bodies of Australia.

8. Explore a statement supported by the churches on care for God's Creation and related ecological topics.

The Queensland Churches Environmental Network was established by Queensland Churches Together soon afterwards and held its first meeting in 2012. This has led to similar groups in other Australian States, and at least one group in a regional area centred on Toowoomba. Put another way, the establishment of such groups was designed to enable the Churches together to make their unique voice and position heard on ecological matters. But they all tend to suffer from the common problem of a lack of funds, and that is difficult especially when trying to operate at a national level. The combination of a large land mass, relatively small population and a voluntary group of busy people stretched across the continent is not conducive to a highly productive group; however it is at least a beginning.

The Role of Peak Organisations

Peak organisations are "umbrella" groups that bring other related groups together or offer assistance and resources, and which therefore have an important overview role to play in the development of effective eco-mission strategies. But because such groups are not well established in Australia I will refer primarily to the British scene.

The British context includes quite a number of peak Christian environmental groups, and at least some of the more prominent ones may quickly be identified by reference to the Environmental Issues Network, or EIN. This was formed in 1999 by Churches Together in Britain and Ireland as a result of work done by the Arthur Rank organisation, and brings together representatives of various groups and Churches working for the environment. The membership of the EIN includes such groups as A Rocha, Eco-Congregation, the John Ray Initiative (JRI), Christian Ecology Link, Operation Noah, the Anglican Church, the Methodist Church, the United Reformed Church, the Salvation Army, Tear Fund, Christian Aid, and representatives of other Churches and groups. In a positive sense it seems to me that the EIN plays an important role in fulfilling its main purpose, which is to share information and to provide coordination so as to try to prevent overlap. But on the other hand such a plethora of groups invariably raises an important question.

Are there too many peak groups in the UK, resulting in excessive overlap and duplication of effort? The probability is that this question cannot be definitively answered, and it certainly cannot be done without reference to context. My hunch is that the answer may be "yes", although I have not found a great deal of evidence to suggest that it is perceived to be a problem in the UK. The issue at stake is that if there are too many peak groups in Britain, it is a pattern that should be treated with some caution before being repeated within the Australian context.

In a conversation with EcoCongregation's Jo Rathbone in 2007 she reflected that "each organisation has a particular niche", while A Rocha's Dave Bookless told me that "if we are wasting resources" or "wasting our time competing with each other rather than getting change where it's needed, then that would worry me." For him, the key is that the groups are talking and working together in a complementary fashion, which is undoubtedly important. While there may be an element of rationalisation in such responses, to some extent a defence of the British peak groups may nevertheless be justified in that the groups tend to reflect different bases and goals.

The primary purpose of these groups is often very similar, namely to support and encourage eco-mission within the Church at large, and in some cases to engage the wider community with the need for change in the way we regard the natural environment. At that level, in the provision of resources for congregations, there is clearly some overlap, and therefore a case to answer. Such a perception is compounded when the role of some denominations is included. One academic referred to what he described as "a major overlap"; in lauding the Eco-Congregation program, he asserted off the record that "none of the denominations have really got behind it", and in some cases they have set up other schemes fulfilling a similar function. "They (the Church of England) would have been better to get in behind Eco-Congregation and putting money into that rather than setting up their own".

When the peak groups are considered in closer detail in terms of their particular goals and fields of operation, a number of differences emerge. Some groups are difficult to categorise, but broadly they can be divided into four main groupings. First, the John Ray Initiative (JRI) probably stands alone in that it serves a particular function at an elite academic level, although it touches a wider audience through its conferences. Second, there are groups that relate to congregations, most notably EcoCongregation, but also A Rocha, the "Church Times" Green Church Award, and the Conservation Foundation. Third, there are groups that tend to operate at a more individual or program level, such as Christian Ecology Link, Operation Noah, or Shrinking the Footprint. Fourth, there are Aid groups such as Christian Aid or the Tear Fund, with a significant ecological edge to their work.

But several quite different groupings emerge when they are considered in terms of their confessional basis. It is interesting that some of the more prominent peak groups in the UK have an Evangelical base. A key question therefore relates to the extent to which the confessional basis of some of the groups may be an advantage or a disadvantage. As I have previously suggested, there is no obvious perception of difficulty, in that the materials and issues covered are very basic and relate specifically to the natural environment. There is an enormous area of consensus in the broad mainstream of ecotheology, even if there are some minor differences of emphasis or expression. Further, the issues involved are invariably practical in nature; it is also important to maintain the integrity of the eco-mission program in general at a peak level.

It is impossible to predict the outcome of any significant increase in the number of religious eco-networks. In a positive sense it could have the effect of increasing the exposure of people to the message of creation care, in that people tend to move in particular circles, and may not be open to influence from sources they do not know or necessarily trust. Evangelicals, for example, may be more influenced by a group like A Rocha, or by a visiting Evangelical from the United States than by a website like the Climate Institute. The danger is that the efforts and limited resources of people and groups may be spread too thinly and thus dissipated.

A number of crucial questions emerge from an analysis of the peak groups, but the fact remains that the potential or actual eco-congregation in Britain has a range of support systems and resources readily available to it. In contrast with that, in relative terms the equivalent Australian congregation does not have access to the same level of support. We are operating too much within our own isolated groupings, and lack the added dimension that an effective peak group support system could offer.

To the best of my knowledge, there is currently no high profile, widely representative and truly effective peak group operating in Australia to promote Christian eco-mission. Moreover, there is strong anecdotal evidence that while some groups are aware of others, and cross-referencing takes place on websites, there is a significant lack of networking nationally. I contend that there are two essential points here. First, it is important that Australia can learn from overseas experience, and not repeat any models that are inappropriate in our context. Second, at the very least it is imperative that something akin to the British Environmental Issues Network should evolve or be established in order to enhance communication, to reduce overlapping and to improve overall effectiveness.

The Possibilities of International Dialogue

It is quite clear that the context for eco-mission varies considerably from one region to another, and even more from one continent to another. Nevertheless I contend that there are a number of ways in which Churches at all levels can help and encourage one another in this important endeavour. At a very basic level, inter-continental dialogue is a reminder that the issues involved are of a global nature, and we are all in it together. Response strategies may vary, but because matters such as climate change and biodiversity have broad implications, it is possible that programs can be developed at the same global level.

But in addition, any feeling of isolation on the part of Australian congregations could be reduced dramatically by awareness of a group such as Interfaith Power and Light in the United States, which is an eco-faith network involving over 10,000 congregations in 39 states – and that is just one organisation in one country. Eco-mission is still at an early stage of its evolution in Australia, and so while it is premature to speculate on the contribution Australia could make to the world church, the uniqueness of our context and environment should ensure that Australian voices will have a contribution to make.

It is of course quite impossible simply to transpose a British or American *modus operandi* into an Australian context, and that it is neither feasible nor desirable to try to replicate in Australia every overseas peak group. At the same time there are several ways in which the Australian Church can learn from overseas approaches and experience.

In the first instance that will involve returning to a similar point of beginning, namely issues of need and context. But this is a theological and not just a pragmatic issue. The vital connection is in the Practical Theology approach that I outlined in Chapter 2 and in the importance of the contextual dimension of Theology. Against that background, it is clear that Australia has a unique geographic, demographic, and social context. It follows therefore that the number and type of peak groups that may be formed should emerge from the context in which they are set. Such an approach may have a higher degree of theological integrity than may otherwise be the case; it does not need to ignore overseas experience, but it may involve grappling with crucial questions emerging from that experience, and an openness to learn from the mistakes of others by choosing not to replicate them in Australia. Nevertheless, some structures for the encouragement of eco-mission may in fact be adapted legitimately from overseas models.

Further analysis may provide additional clarification, but in brief, the first presence of appropriate peak groups is both important and needed in Australia. At the same time, I would argue that because of the degree of consensus on ecological issues not only across the usual Christian divisions, but also across the broader religious divisions, a narrowly defined confessional basis is problematic.

Issues relating to local congregations and individuals represent the main "grey area", and it is there that the most careful consideration will be required. It may be that a degree of market economics applies here, but the most effective outcome, I believe, will result from a careful consideration of what support or encouragement systems are needed in the diverse Australian context, and that will involve looking primarily at the larger good than at our own preferred theological emphasis. Thus, my contention is that something as fundamental as the future of life on the planet will require a high degree of cooperation between Christian denominations, other world religions, and community and government agencies, for the good of all.

The Role of Eco Awards

There is another important support mechanism that helps to reduce feelings of isolation, and that is in the role of eco awards. We look first at how that works in several overseas locations. In the UK the peak organisation EcoCongregation has had an important role in encouraging eco-mission at a local level in that country, both through the resources it provides and the incentive offered by the Eco Award. Although it operates with very limited staff, its impact is nevertheless significant. When the group was first formed, funding was available for a fulltime position; that person was the Rev Dr David Pickering, who prior to ordination had gained a PhD in environmental chemistry. Pickering set up the system of eco awards, and prepared a comprehensive resource base of 12 modules, beginning with a "Church Check Up", but going on to cover a wide range of relevant material and ideas to which congregations could refer.

What that meant was that a congregation intent on setting out to do eco-mission was not alone. Jane, as a member of the St Leonard's Nottingham group, picked up that point in her observation that "you can email Jo (at EcoCongregation) and ask questions or if there's something you're struggling with you can ask advice; you can ask about material or books to tap into, so I think it is really useful"[21]. There was a resource, a person to contact, and a clear challenge. I found that congregations were generally appreciative of this facility and resource.

An Eco Award is applicable for a three year period, which means that a congregation is encouraged to take further steps in eco-mission in order to reapply. The Bethesda Methodist Church in Cheltenham is illustrative of what that can mean. Barrett stated, "A few people, maybe even half at the beginning, weren't that aware of the award but thought that working for the environment was something we should be doing. Once we got the award people became very proud – pleased that they had done it, pleased they had got it, and said 'That's a mark of what we've done'. And Mark Barrett would say, 'yes, but what next?' And the thought of not achieving the eco award would upset a lot of people"[22]. Thus, for them it became a sign of something they had done, steps they had taken, and it led to that

---

21 Interview 2007.
22 Interview 2007.

congregation encouraging other congregations in the area to take steps in the same direction.

When a congregation believes it has fulfilled the requirements for the Award, an application is made to EcoCongregation. Several independent assessors then visit the congregation, and depending on their judgment, the Award may be given, and that is current for three years. Thus, the Award structure provides a resource for learning and development in eco-mission, and since it is for a period of three years, it becomes a tool of encouragement to continue on a journey. The key here is accountability and the encouragement to work through the material. The other aspect to be considered is that it enables a congregation to indicate publicly that it is an eco congregation, and has been judged to be thus by an independent panel.

I found that congregations employed different methods in displaying their award. St Chad's, for example, set the plaque into the ground in its natural churchyard area. Others were displayed in a more visible setting. One notable example is Christchurch Baptist-Methodist Church in Leicester, which has two Eco Awards prominently displayed at the Church entrance. One cannot get so far as the porch of the building without being made aware that this is an eco congregation. A further somewhat similar example is the case of Bethesda Methodist at Cheltenham, where in addition to the Award display, there are strategically placed signs on the top of bins or items in the kitchen, reminding people that this is an eco congregation, and therefore the people should respond in certain ways. There is evidence that eco considerations are in play in every facet of their congregational life, and that their eco-mission activity has led to a number of people coming into the life of the Church as it has engaged with the community.

A somewhat similar system operates in South Africa through the Southern African Faith Communities Environmental Institute, or SAFCEI as it is known, which is very active in promoting Earthcare in an inter-faith context. Its Eco-congregations program seeks to do a number of things. Like its British EcoCongregation equivalent it provides a handbook with a guiding framework, links a congregation into a network, provides resources, and ultimately a certificate award.

The situation in Australia is somewhat different. The Five Leaf Eco Award scheme founded by Jessica Morthorpe sets out to be "an ecumenical behaviour change program for churches" with the aim to "provide a reward for churches working towards environmental sustainability and an incentive and the resources for churches to do more"[23]. The Five Leaf Scheme appears to operate on a slightly different basis from its overseas counterparts; certainly, as the website indicates, it aims to make a practical difference. My impression is that it does not yet have a high profile within the Australian Church, and this remains one of the on-going challenges in the promotion of full-orbed eco-mission in Australia. Among other things, in my view any award scheme needs to include the theological and Biblical base as well as networking eco-congregations.

Some may choose not to go down the award path; many of the people with whom I spoke were wary of such an idea which to them appeared like a reward for action taken on behalf of the environment. Of course one does not engage in eco-mission for the sake of an award, but there are two factors in particular that need to be considered. The first is that a fundamental part of the Award approach is the provision of resources that a congregation is able to work through. This material must contain ideas, questions and information that people are encouraged to address in a way that leads to action. Thus, it remains a significant possibility in the movement towards effective eco-mission.

Dealing with Negativity

But how do we respond to the probability of some negativity when it comes to environmental matters, including the Churches' involvement? How do we deal with climate change deniers who seem to think that having dispatched climate change they are thereby absolved from the need to care for the Earth, or that a liveable environment would be good to have providing the economy can afford it? I know that personally I have had emails (fortunately not many!) that have fairly made my blood boil. But there can also be negativity around the issue of how little the Church seems to be doing in environmental care. The short answer, I believe, is to stay positive; stay with a positive agenda and don't waste precious emotional energy on a debate that you will never win. In spite of a multiplicity of official Statements there have always been some dissenting voices, and while a divided voice invariably weakens the efforts of the Church as a whole, the

---

23 See eg http://greenchurch.victas.uca.org.au/

case should not be overstated either. The answer to negativity is passionate and committed positivity!

Conclusion

Sometimes we can become so caught up in our particular local issues that we lose sight of "the big picture"; but there is no shortage of material from national and international ecumenical and denominational sources to provide a significant consensus about Earthcare. We can all draw strength and encouragement from that.

I have considered the nature and significant role of what I am calling peak groups, especially as they operate in the UK; that led me to ask whether there may be too many such groups in Britain, and to raise some concern about the possible influence of confessional issues. The opposite problem exists in Australia where there is a shortage of prominent and effective peak groups, but we might learn from overseas experience. Further, I have considered the role of denominational hierarchies, which can have an important bearing on eco-mission programs in local congregations and have suggested that a well constructed eco award scheme can make a positive difference.

There is always the danger of a gap developing between official statements and specific action either at a local or any other level; the key issue for the next chapter is therefore an exploration of what eco-mission looks like on the ground, and in order to do that we will use both British and Australian examples. There is still much we can learn and do in response to the global ecological crisis and the imperative to care for creation at the heart of the Christian Faith.

CHAPTER SEVEN

Eco-mission in Action

We have considered some of the theological dimensions of eco-mission, or mission with an earth flavour, based on a sound eco-theology. But for such a theology to have any meaning, it must find its expression in a genuine and practical way. It is at this point that Forrester's "hermeneutic spiral" which I mentioned in Chapter 2 becomes poignant: "engagement and understanding interact with one another to seek a strengthening of commitment, a reform of the Church, and a more just and caring social order, which will reflect the coming reign of God"[1]. It would be difficult to find a more precise expression of the basic issue.

Sooner or later the central question of how theology relates to the practical issues of eco-mission gives rise to a range of subsequent questions, which opens up an enormous field. For example, what is the role of context in eco-mission? What does an Australian eco-congregation look like? How does one balance local and global aspects of eco-theology and eco-mission?

My quest for answers to such questions took me to England, on the basis that there was known eco-mission in that country, with a variety of Churches that would describe themselves as "eco congregations", together with a well-established supporting structure at a peak level. Moreover, since I had lived and worked in the UK for a year, I considered that my relative familiarity with the country and its Churches would enable research to be more productive; but having said that, the main focus of my work was always going to be the Australian context.

Clearly, as we have previously noted, context is a vital dimension; and the British context is in many respects quite different from its Australian counterpart. This is a very obvious point that does not need to be laboured here, but one could cite some of the more obvious examples. At a basic level, Britain has a small land mass with a relatively large population, which means that communities are generally more compact, and the capacity to maintain support services is thereby enhanced. The climate is also obviously

---

1 Forrester, *Truthful Action, 30.*

very different from that in Australia. In terms of eco-mission possibilities, there are several less obvious factors. Recycling is conducted in a rather different way to Australia, and it may seem that it becomes a more complex operation in Britain. Many British churches also have quite extensive grounds, including community cemeteries that must be maintained by the Church. When that fact is taken into account alongside other factors, it becomes clear that the praxis of eco-mission must be worked out in a particular context, and cannot simply be transferred from one situation to another. Nevertheless, in this chapter I will again be drawing on both British and Australian experience and examples.

Attitudes

Given their interest in ecotheology and mission, it is hardly surprising that virtually all the respondents in my research expressed basic attitudes that were consistent with the stance adopted by national and ecumenical Church bodies. Similarly, it is to be expected that they would reflect community concerns as well.

All respondents stated their belief, even their strong belief, that the global environmental situation is serious, and further, that the crisis is becoming increasingly evident in Australia. It may be noted that the Church leaders I was able to interview all stated similar views strongly, even though few of them had any involvement in eco-mission. One would expect that to be a significant motivating factor for Christian environmental activists; but it is self-evident that such a unanimous position does not necessarily translate into support for the proposition from ordinary Church members, let alone practical action, but the degree of concern evident in the community as a whole would suggest that any problem with Christian eco-mission resides elsewhere.

A wide range of particular issues were identified as concerns within the Australian context. The most common concern related to water, which also extended to the Murray-Darling river system. Other concerns included the on-going use of coal-fired power stations, the shortage of funds for the development of renewable energy, an obsession with petrol prices combined with an increase in road traffic and the lack of public transport. However, as I have suggested, respondents also raised numerous other issues, which demonstrates not only that Christian people are thinking about these matters, but also they are reflecting local as well as global concerns. There were fewer indications of hope regarding the overall environmental situation, but perceptibly there is a rise in the level of interest and awareness among the population at large.

One noteworthy point was the strong support for the notion that environmental action, or the care of creation, should be part of the Church's mission. The Questionnaire included the statement, "From a theological perspective, creation care should be part of the Church's mission"; all respondents agreed, and most agreed strongly. Such an affirmation on the part of those who are attempting to engage in eco-mission is not surprising. However, the point of interest is the fact that even some of those who are not currently engaged in or promoting eco-mission believe that this is a valid expression of Christian mission, and is by no means an optional extra. I contend that this reflects one of the central problems facing eco-mission in Australia. There is a significant inconsistency involved, a disconnection between accepted theory and actual practice. The challenge is to reduce or eliminate such a gap.

How Eco-mission Begins

It is clear that eco-mission does not have a long history in Australia, but nevertheless it is necessary to ask how it begins in a local or congregational setting. In answer to that, a study of some initiatives will be instructive. As I will demonstrate, it will require a catalyst of some kind, either in the form of an event which is created, or one that takes place and requires a response or interpretation. In order to illustrate that point, I will relate briefly the stories of five congregations, each of which in its own way informs the progress of eco-mission in Australia. Those congregations are at Caloundra and Stafford in Queensland, Northmead and Maroubra Junction in New South Wales, and Scots Church in South Australia.

One congregation that I know reasonably well and that has embarked on an eco-mission agenda is the Caloundra Uniting Church on the Sunshine Coast of Queensland; and since I was part of that development, it provides a good case study. The congregation is what some would style as a "program church", in that it has a worshipping congregation of about 150, and consequently a variety of groups. One significant feature is that a Social Justice group has been operating there for a number of years, and in recent times that has included active support for a non-Christian refugee family. Such a combination of circumstances was therefore conducive to an environmental concern.

The catalyst or beginning point was the moment when the Chair of the Social Justice group suggested to me that we might do something in this area of concern. I agreed, and we quickly reached a decision that I would present an eco-seminar at the Church. The initial plan was to invite members of the community as well, but subsequently it was decided (wisely, I believe) that for this first attempt the seminar should be limited to the people of the Church. Thus, the various congregations in the region were invited. The seminar was held in October 2007 with about 24 in attendance; the ground covered included the nature of the problem, eco-theology, a theology of eco-mission, my findings from a visit to the UK, and a discussion of what further steps could be taken as Churches in the area.

The response to the seminar was positive, and led to several outcomes. Most notably it provided a platform for the Social Justice group to discuss a future eco-mission program for the Caloundra Church. Ideas were discussed in the meetings that were held over succeeding months, so that a core group of approximately 10 committed people emerged.

Another "light on the hill" is St Clements-on-the-Hill Anglican Church at Stafford in Brisbane. Their eco journey began in 2004 with the arrival of a new Rector, the Rev Mary Florence. She had made it clear prior to the confirmation of her appointment that this was a key issue for her. At the same time, there was a small group of concerned people who were ready to engage this issue along with the Rector.

The story of the Northmead congregation began in about 1998 when a number of people, including the Minister, noticed that an area adjacent to the Church, including a creek and bushland, was in need of regeneration. They decided to adopt one section of it, and worked on it on a monthly basis, a process that involved cooperation with the local Council and assistance with plants. A walking track was created to a children's park. The congregation regarded this work as part of their Christian witness, and interestingly the work of the Uniting Church was publicly acknowledged. From that initial awareness some forms of eco-theological and eco-mission awareness have emerged, including the employment of a part-time ministry worker whose brief includes the encouragement of bush walking and creation spirituality.

Maroubra Junction has become a congregation of strategic importance in the development of eco-mission within the Uniting Church in New South Wales. Its genesis was a conversation between two members of the congregation after worship one Sunday morning. They agreed that care of the environment should be part of the Church's mission. A phone call was made to the local Council, and from that beginning Maroubra's eco-mission has grown.

In 2005 an eco-faith community began in Adelaide in association with Scots Uniting Church in the city. The Rev Dr Jason John was initially appointed as a Consultant to Scots Church for 6 months with the aim of exploring possible links between the Church and the nearby University. However, that led to John proposing that the Church should relate to the whole eco agenda; at the time he was proposing to return to New South Wales, but when a number of people expressed interest, he was appointed for a trial period of two years. John saw his eco-ministry being shaped around six issues – justice, spirituality, companioning or pastoral care, theology, embryonic permaculture communities, and worship or contemplation.

But the catalyst that provides a point of beginning can also be a seemingly small everyday event. For several people in the Anglican Church at Wacol it was twofold. First, an unconfined church cat killed a native bird in full view of the worshipping congregation, and second, a very weedy church property and a priest who was apparently defensive of the serious weeds. At Holland Park Uniting Church it was the changing of light bulbs; the message there, to borrow a British phrase, is "don't stop at the lights!"

The motivation for commencing an eco-mission program in a congregation almost invariably has its genesis in the passion of a particular individual. In some cases that person was a member of the clergy. In the case of Holy Trinity Skipton, the clear perception is that it was the regional Bishop whose drive and commitment led not only to the formation of a group but also to eco-activity in the Diocese. Holy Trinity at Cleeve traces the beginning to the Vicar, who was impressed by a book she read at the age of 13. In acknowledging that the initiative rose out of her own history, the Vicar Cathy said she knew there were several other people in the congregation "who were equally passionate about the environment, so I knew it wasn't just going to be 'a Vicar thing'[2]". Somewhat similar stories could be told of Derby and Leicester.

The Rector of the Church of the Ascension at Ealing traced the point of beginning to a member of the congregation, who "was very strong on saying we need to pick up this environment agenda and do something with it". He continued, "I had by a different route come to a conviction that this also was important, so it was a mixing of minds I suppose at the right point...[3]". The story of Bethesda Methodist in Cheltenham was different again. The Minister, Mark Barrett, indicated that "one of the things that brought it (the environmental issue) to bear in our own church was the action in China to dam up the rivers and alter the course of major rivers for industrialisation purposes"[4]. This led to the thought that humans could change, perhaps adversely, what God had created.

The essential point here is that in terms of making a start in eco-mission, "the power and passion of one" is of great importance. The evidence points to the conclusion that in many cases, all it takes is for one person, or at most a very small core of people, to have the vision and drive to say "this is important, and we should do this."

Issues to Note

Before considering eco-mission themes in more detail, there are three issues of a general nature within the British context that should be noted. These relate to motivation, and the respective roles of local "Green Teams" and of the clergy, although it may become apparent that these themes are inter-related. The implications for the Australian Church are clear.

Once an eco-mission agenda has been established, a small "green team" almost invariably becomes the "nerve centre", motivator, and enabler of eco-mission in the congregation. The EcoCongregation organisation in Britain with which all the congregations I visited are associated, requires the appointment of someone they call the "Green Apostle", and that person obviously becomes the local group convenor; some of those people are particularly gifted and active beyond the local congregation as well. I had

---

2 Interview 2007.
3 Interview 2007.
4 Interview 2007.

the opportunity to meet with a number of those groups. Some were small but effective, such as at Skipton; others were larger, such as at St Chad's in Leeds or St Leonard's in Nottingham. Even at St Leonard's, where I met with perhaps 18 interested people, the driving force may still be traced to a small inner core group.

Rightly or wrongly, the role of the clergy is also perceived to be important. In some cases, such as the smaller congregation at Derby, the role of the Rector, Canon Donald Macdonald, and his wife as the key drivers or enablers of the eco-mission is significant. This was strengthened by Macdonald's Diocesan role. Similarly in the Church at Ealing, the combination of a strong lay leader and a committed clergyperson is obviously powerful and effective. In many of the effective eco-congregations though, the model is one of an active lay group working with the full encouragement and support of the clergy, but it is not clergy-driven. Skipton is a good example of that; a group member said, "… we wouldn't have set up the group here if Adrian (the Rector) hadn't been supportive"[5]. St Leonard's in Nottingham is another example of effective lay-clergy cooperation; I personally attended an environmentally-focussed worship service at St Leonard's, in which the Rector emphatically declared, "We are an eco-congregation".

In other cases, however, where eco-mission does not necessarily have the full and active support of the clergyperson, the work of the core group is just that much harder, and probably less effective than it might be. The mission of a congregation does not have to be clergy-driven, but the active support and appropriate leadership of the clergy is clearly a real bonus and a strong encouragement for the congregation as a whole to become involved in the eco-mission agenda. This is reflected both in perceptions of morale and the degree of congregational support.

Eco Groups

Stories of the beginning of eco-mission in congregations could be multiplied, but from what I have related, and reflecting on both the Australian and the British experience, a number of factors start to become apparent. The first and arguably most important factor is the presence of one or two key people who are committed to an eco-mission agenda or who are prepared to make an issue of the environment, and consequently to begin to exert

---

5 Interview 2007.

some leadership. That in turn almost invariably leads to the development of a small group with an on-going life as the focus of eco-mission in the congregation. Thus, since it is clear that an eco-mission initiative invariably involves a core group of some kind, often combined with one or more key individuals, it is worth considering the role of such groups, and asking what it is that makes a group work. A number of factors appear to emerge from the stories related above.

It is helpful if at least one of the emerging eco leaders has some expertise or initiative in the field. At Caloundra, for example, there were several people apart from me who had a strong ecological commitment, which in one case combined with professional expertise in the process of environmental audits, while another member of the group had a postgraduate qualification in theology. This provided a depth of background that was extremely helpful in developing a workable approach, and it suggests that the availability of local expertise could be especially important in the many situations where feelings of isolation seriously inhibit the possibility of effective work.

The size of the core group obviously varies, and at times it can be very small. Coordination at the Maroubra Junction Uniting Church was in the hands of three people, although a dozen people became involved. On the other hand, Northmead Uniting had a core group of about 20 people, Caloundra had 12, and the Anglican Church at Logan had 25 people. In other cases the size of the group varied. However, if the British experience is any guide, it will be important for the larger groups especially to have a small coordinating group, or even a particular person charged with the responsibility of enabling the direction of the group as a whole.

The perceived level of support from the congregation as a whole varies considerably. In some cases, such as Northmead and Logan, the support level was high. In other cases, the support was only moderate, while in other situations it could be described as poor. In some of those situations the eco-mission in the congregation may be largely or even solely confined to the small group, as was the case at Denistone East Uniting Church, where the core group consisted of 7 people. In other cases the congregation may offer little more than moral support, as in the case of the Clarence Uniting Church in Tasmania where the Minister was a doctoral candidate in an eco-related field. However, the hope is always that the core group will become the means by which eco-mission is able to operate in the congregation as a whole.

Morale is something that is not easy to measure or quantify, and one must differentiate between the feelings of the core group and their satisfaction rating so far as the congregation is concerned. Morale in the core group is often very high, but frequently that does not translate into satisfaction about achievements in the congregation.

In summary, while there are no universal principles involved, a number of factors generally accompany the commencement of an eco-mission approach in a congregation. First, I have noted the significance of one or several key people who are willing and able to take the initiative and give the necessary early leadership. Second, that initiative is often associated with the formation of a small core group that will effectively enable goals to be set and achieved. A further point, building on the previous two, is that some kind of catalyst may be needed in order to create a basis for beginning.

Beyond that, it is helpful if the congregation has developed a social conscience that includes the human dimension but extends beyond it. And finally, it is also helpful if the congregation is of a sufficient size to have a variety of groups operating, so that it is more likely to have leaders available to undertake a role in eco-mission. However, that is not to say that a small congregation is unable to participate.

Mission Statements

As in the British context, it is noteworthy that very often congregations do not perceive the importance of a specific Mission Statement related to the care of creation. The existence of such a Statement obviously does not guarantee effective eco-mission, but on the other hand the absence of such a document, inherent in an *ad hoc* approach, significantly increases the probability that the congregation or group involved has not thought through the vision and goals that underlie their endeavours. Others import a statement from elsewhere. Thus, Anglican congregations associated with AngliGreen in Brisbane tended to refer to the Mission Statement of that group, while Uniting Church congregations in the Sydney North area tended to refer to the Earth Ministry Statement. Such an approach is not necessarily illegitimate; the vision and aims of eco-mission will to a large extent reflect the general theological under-pinning of such an endeavour, while the goals that emerge will tend to vary according to the particular context in which it is set. But what is of crucial importance is for the Statement to be truly "owned" by the congregation. One way in which that may be encouraged is for a group to work through any proposed Mission Statement, and even more by presenting the Statement to the congregation for their response. As an example, Caloundra's Mission Statement emerged out of a seminar and the consequent discussion within the Social Justice group. The fact that the Caloundra congregation voted to accept the Mission Statement clearly has on-going implications for ownership and accountability.

The Statement recognises a threefold Vision, followed by three objectives, and is based on the recognition of the natural environment as God's Creation. The Vision affirms that:

- "Christians are called to safeguard the integrity of Creation, and to exercise their mission in such a way that the life of the earth is sustained and renewed.

- Alongside other valid expressions of Christian mission, the proclamation of the Kingdom of God includes working for justice, peace, and a proper stewardship of the earth.

- The well-being of people is inter-woven with the well-being of the planet itself."

In response to that vision, the ecological aims of the Church are:

- "To raise environmental awareness in the congregation and throughout the community.

- To engage in practical measures on behalf of the environment.

- To encourage a form of spirituality that includes an appreciation and care for Creation."

Clearly, specific goals will rise out of the Vision and Objectives. To facilitate and implement the objectives and goals, and to assist the congregation in caring for creation, a core group of interested persons may be established as a sub-group of the Social Justice Group. Decisions that affect the congregation will be made on a shared basis under the authority of the Church Council, and will be in keeping with Synod policies. Obviously it is still early in the life of this emerging group of "eco warriors", but a start has been made.

The Power of One

Another significant aspect that is worth noting from some of the data and stories of eco-mission initiatives indicated above is what could be called "the power of one", or the capacity of one individual, or perhaps a very small group, to begin a chain reaction involving other people, thereby making a substantial difference. In addition to some individuals noted in those stories, some other notable examples may be cited briefly. Dr Jason John's initiative led to an eco-congregation in Adelaide, and that in turn contributed to his ground-breaking appointment as an Eco-Minister in a New South Wales Presbytery. Also in New South Wales, a very small group led to an association with Professor Barry Leal in what became the Earth Ministry and the WaterLines project in North Sydney. What can one person do? The brief answer is, quite a lot, especially if that person has some expertise in the area.

A second demonstration of "the power of one" is in terms of what one congregation is able to achieve. Thus, one positive outcome from the eco seminar at Caloundra has been the possibility of eco-mission emerging in some neighbouring congregations.

Themes in Local Eco-Mission

What then does eco-mission look like at a local level? The matter of what can be achieved is illustrated in the stories that may be told, and because of the potential number of those I need to be selective. However, while eco congregations in Britain generally have quite well established programs, it is arguable that their scope tends to be somewhat limited. Comparatively, eco-mission in Australia appears to be at an earlier stage of development, and consequently the number of eco-projects is limited, which means that any conclusions must be tentative. Nevertheless, while it is not yet clear what a mature outcome might be, and a degree of caution is appropriate, some patterns are beginning to emerge. I believe that nine significant themes may be identified at this stage. Some of these reflect a similar pattern to that in Britain, although there are differences.

Worship

The inclusion of ecology in worship is predictably and appropriately one of the more common themes, and there is no shortage of resources available on the internet in particular. Some of those are from overseas sources, and therefore they may need to be adapted. The other significant drawback is that busy clergy may not always stop to seek out the material, and would be helped by encouragement from a central source, in terms of a reminder of an appropriate occasion, such as World Environment Day, and by something that is placed in their hands.

An increasing number of Churches are using the "Season of Creation" material as a resource; this initiative traces back to Norman Habel, a South Australia Lutheran, although the scope of the material is obviously ecumenical in character. Briefly, Churches are encouraged to use four Sundays in September leading up to St Francis of Assisi Day in order to celebrate the natural world, or God's creation. The website contains a significant and valuable volume of resource material, including lectionary readings, liturgies, stories, theology, sermons, and much more. Such a concentration of eco-worship in one month of the year, by contrast with a more seasonal approach in Britain, has its advantages and disadvantages. Congregations and clergy will make up their own minds; but it may be argued that a seasonal approach is generally less appropriate in Australia. On the other hand, a concentrated approach may miss taking advantage of an event such as World Environment Day unless an effort was made to include creation issues in the liturgy from time to time during the year.

In addition to a variety of adult study programs, something of a pattern appears to be developing across many British congregations, involving the development of 4 or 5 special services each year, as well as references in the liturgy on other occasions. Simon Reed at Ealing argued a case for eco-worship to be related to the seasons of the year, but others focussed more on special events or Sundays, such as Harvest Festival, Rogation, or World Environment Day. Many congregations reported regular preaching on appropriate eco themes, while other initiatives include approaches to Celtic spirituality and Prayer Walks.

The Bramford Road Methodist Church reported an innovative approach to worship in the following terms:

> *Church members in Ipswich were shocked when they arrived for worship. It was as if a waste bin had been emptied and its contents strewn around the church. Inspired by the large Cornish attraction, the all-age service had the theme of 'The Eden Project'. During the service, the world was described as the garden of God and we have been placed in the garden to look after it. To the*

relief of worried worshippers, our young people then tidied up the church and collected all the rubbish. Of course, the rubbish was not collected to be thrown away, but bagged for recycling.[6]

A practical approach to worship was also adopted by Wanstead URC with a "worship in wellies" service. People were invited to come to worship in their best gardening attire; after the service and a picnic lunch they set to work on cleaning up the Church grounds. Many congregations reported such activities as a "Walk to Church" Sunday, the provision of eco resources, a display on water use, and information on recycling.

Children and Youth

In some ways and in some congregations in particular, this is an area of strength. St Leonard's Nottingham is one example of some quite extensive and creative children's work. Beyond the obvious lessons with an environmental theme, some of the teaching is taken outdoors in summer. The 4 to 6 year-olds had a "sad earth, happy earth" session, and even at that age were introduced to trade justice and poverty issues. Older children were involved in a "living water" session and a "helping hands map of Africa", while the 11 to 16 years age group worked on a drama on care of creation, were involved in "creation" services, and prepared a youth service with drama on the life of St Francis.

Some of the teaching of course involved activity, such as the making of posters, gardens, involvement in recycling, the selling of Fairtrade products, and using recycled materials. St John's at Swansea had a creative Noah's Ark project, while Leicester Methodists took their young people to the well-equipped community-based Environment Education Centre. St Mary the Virgin Church in Durham enabled the children to build a dolls house size eco-house from cardboard; this formed part of a display, "and was hailed as a model of good practice". Some fun approaches to learning about the environment have also been developed; for example, Northallerton United Reformed Church used Operation Noah in that way, while Torphichen Church in Scotland has developed a fun approach to learning with eco-bingo and an environmental version of snakes and ladders. In addition, they stated "We visit Edinburgh Zoo annually to learn about breeding programs for endangered species and we now sponsor the Asiatic lions. We

---

6 EcoCongregation website, accessed 2009.

made our own t-shirts with the words 'Going, Going, Gone' depicting two endangered species on the front ('Going') and an extinct one on the back ('Gone')", which apparently made quite an impression at the Zoo.

Spirituality

Spirituality is a related area that is still in the process of development; Tasmania offers several examples. When Paul Chalson was in Hobart he ran a project he called "Earth Pilgrimage"; in his words, "Essentially it is a journey through and into a place which involves times of becoming attentively aware both of the place within which we journey and God present in and through this place," so that it is in effect "a mixture of a bushwalk, a worship service and a spiritual retreat.[7]" But significantly this approach included a monthly eco-worship service which was co-led by the pastor of an indigenous congregation; it also had an educational dimension.

Margy Dockray in Launceston works largely on her own in encouraging creation or eco-spirituality. However, she has an ambitious plan involving 400 acres of "stunning wet native forest", some of it over 300 years old, and with numerous other natural features including a virtual botanic garden. She has a plan to link these features with walking and riding trails, and to incorporate a "memorial forest" where people can bury the ashes of deceased loved ones in a natural setting. Dockray states, "Ultimately I would like the land to be a place of healing, by developing a retreat centre, community garden and dedicated worship space, with inter-faith links. I believe this could be a way to reach the great unchurched majority of the population.[8]"

Spirituality is also emerging as a significant issue in a number of Anglican Churches. St Clement's Church at Stafford has converted a grassy slope into a native vegetation area in order to make a statement about the God of creation. Nearby is a community garden, complete with poultry, which it must be acknowledged is rare in a Church. St Phillip's Church at Annerley has also created a green space where people can wander and meditate; Biblical and spiritual prompts are strategically located at various points of the garden. Initiatives such as these are a powerful reminder of the way in which people may be encouraged to relate life and faith to the natural world.

---

7 Personal communication.
8 Personal communication.

Policy Issues

Another area might be labelled as policy issues; this includes a number of different dimensions. An environmental audit features strongly here, and can produce some surprising results, but always with the potential to improve the Church's environmental performance. Clearly that needs to be monitored regularly for it to be effective. The framing of eco-mission policy is also important, together with seeking of grants for environmental projects and other possibilities. A related area centres on buildings and property, including design features. The new Wesley House in Brisbane is one example of design with the environment in mind. Energy features as an issue for many congregations, usually in terms of monitoring its use, turning off unnecessary lights, installing low energy bulbs, and having an efficient cooling or heating system.

The generation of renewable energy is one area that has undergone rapid expansion in recent years with the installation of solar PV cells on Church roofs. There are numerous examples, but one that has attracted its share of attention has been the 4.2 kilowatt installation in the form of a cross on the Caloundra Uniting Church. It was not the first and it is certainly not the largest, but the solar cross is impossible to miss from the road, and it represents a powerful statement by the Church. There are two possible dangers here; the first is the possibility that a congregation may think that in installing solar panels they have largely done their duty to the environment, and the second is that it may be done largely for financial purposes. Such an installation is a good beginning, but it is only a beginning, and it needs to be done in the context of a larger eco-mission plan.

Other congregations have also taken or are exploring initiatives relating to water use and collection, and this is becoming increasingly important. One outstanding example of this is the Belconnen Baptist Church in the Australian Capital Territory which has installed a 170,000 litre underground rainwater tank.

Church Agencies also have a role to play in the development of effective environmental policies. One such example is UnitingCare and BlueCare, which as agencies of the Queensland Synod of the Uniting Church have developed clear environmental policies that extend to their choice of vehicles, the encouragement of "environmental champions" in each sector of the organisation, and even the use of a slogan such as "be seen in green this World Environment Day".

Prophetic

Social and eco justice are two sides of the one coin, and both are important. In the previous chapter I referred to the Uniting Church response in the form of the booklet "A Just Society" prepared ahead of the 2013 Federal Election in Australia. This may be an uncomfortable area for many local congregations, but the booklet is an example of a production that attempts to crystallise the issues; as such it is the kind of tool that is most useful for the kind of political, commercial, or prophetic pressure that needs to be exercised both by the Church and by individual members, regardless of who is in power. It is difficult to over-emphasize the importance of this issue; in large measure we know what we need to do, but short-term populist politics ensures that there is often a lack of will to do it. We need to re-capture the spirit of the prophets!

Fairtrade is one area in which the British Church appears to be well ahead of the Australian model, although once again the contexts are different. In one form or another it featured quite prominently in British congregations, even among some with no specific eco-mission agenda. An example of the latter is the Chapel Street Methodist Church in Penzance. In some cases, such as the Christchurch Baptist-Methodist Church in Leicester, the Fairtrade stall is not only very prominently placed in the building, but also could be deemed to be successful in two ways. First, in terms of turnover, a local lay leader indicated that over the past 16 years of the program's operation, Fairtrade had grossed £100,000, while it now exceeds £10,000 per year. It should be said that this is one of the larger examples of its kind. One further qualification is that Fairtrade goods also feature quite prominently in many local supermarkets in Britain. Second, and importantly, such a program in a local congregation serves as a constant educational tool. Bethesda Methodist at Cheltenham is a further example of this. Every Sunday there is a prominent Traidgreen stall at the Church, so that this becomes a constant reminder of the inter-related issues involved, as well as providing the opportunity for people to buy a range of goods consistent with the eco approach. Light bulbs are also sold.

Australian examples are harder to find, but some congregations have held a Fairtrade and Green Market day which draws not only the local community, but also related groups as stall holders. Such an event in itself is useful enough, but it is also able to be an educational tool in addition to providing a market that would ultimately assist some vulnerable people.

Community Projects

There have been some important projects that link the Church community with the wider community; among other things this involves the planting of trees and gardens, or the creation of natural vegetation areas. Don Gibson from St Phillip's Church indicated that the Church was located close to a major motor retailer that boasted attractive gardens, and he used this in part as an incentive for the Church to make a statement about its God of creation through the medium of a Church garden. Bush regeneration was one of the significant dimensions of Northmead's eco program, and in that regard they work in cooperation with the local Council. The WaterLines project in Sydney, associated with Earth Ministry when it was operational, encouraged congregations in its area to "adopt a creek", and that approach came with ecotheological educational material. In the same spirit as WaterLines, the Uniting Church Eco-theology Group on the Blackall Range in Queensland undertook a project to clean up Obi Obi Creek.

Community Gardens have become another rapidly expanding outlet for eco-mission in this wider setting. One such project is based at St George's Uniting Church at Eden in southern New South Wales, and appropriately called the Garden of Eden! This is particularly significant in the way it connects diverse factors. The congregation consists of only about 20 worshippers, but over a period of seven years they have been in contact with hundreds of people. It is first and foremost a community garden, but beyond that it connects with Aboriginal people and the unemployed, it holds monthly markets and community lunches, conducts art and cultural activity and much more. They have installed a solar hot water system, a water tank and watering system, along with water courses to educate the community in sustainability. The Rev Judith Dalton, who was Minister in Eden at the time, has written:

> The Garden of Eden was set up as an 'eco-conscious' initiative by people who were already living eco-conscious lifestyles and wanted to share that

with others, and the community responded and developed around it. As stated on the Garden of Eden sign: 'St George's Uniting Church is working with the community to create an eco-conscious and wonder-filled garden and a lively art and cultural centre. Come in ... enjoy ... and connect with the Creator, Earth and all Humanity'[9].

Contact with the wider community takes a number of forms in Britain. For example, Holy Trinity Cleeve works together with the local school to operate a successful "walking bus" to the school. Holy Trinity Skipton has prepared a "Green Pages" directory of local businesses that support environmentally friendly practice; this resource, which includes paid advertising, is made available in the community, and is useful in highlighting both the importance of the eco theme, and the role of the Church in that matter. Lutterworth Methodist reported an Eco Fair, which included stalls and information, and involved the District Council, a library service, and local traders. Outside groups using Church facilities are drawn into the eco circle in several ways, for example through recycling as at Evesham, or through an extension of the Fairtrade stall in the case of Endcliffe Methodist Church. Effective use has also been made of Church Notice boards.

The Church grounds also tend to feature prominently in the eco-mission list in Britain, with many congregations committing to cleaning up their graveyard in particular. It need hardly be said that in this regard there is a major difference between Britain and Australia! This work extends to the provision of wildlife nesting boxes and the making of compost; but it is worth pausing on this issue before moving on. One quite extensive churchyard area is at St Chad's Church in Leeds. Dalton, as leader of the Green Team, said "We started off really getting involved with the Yorkshire Wildlife Trust, and their 'living churchyard'. But as soon as we thought that we could get involved in that, we started looking at EcoCongregation as a whole"[10].

One particularly prominent example of a Church graveyard project is at Saints Mary and John Church at Oxford; the driving force behind this project, which was even featured on the BBC, is Ruth Conway. The grounds are approximately one hectare in size, and as Ruth Conway explained, had become not just a jungle, but "a jungle that was being used for people to hide away, and take drugs and so on"[11]. The goal, which has largely been

---

9 Private email.
10 Interview 2007.
11 Interview 2007.

accomplished, was to transform a forbidding place of criminal activity into "a welcoming, open, quiet green place"[12]. Its easily accessible location is also an advantage. Such a major undertaking gained the cooperation of local community residents, the Council, and Police. More than that, Conway's motivation was not merely to clean up a dangerous area, but it was primarily "to be a way of alerting the congregation to their whole relationship with nature, and with God's good intentions"[13]. This was therefore one of the beginning points for eco-mission in the congregation, and it had implications for worship, spirituality, and outreach to the community.

A variation on the churchyard theme is the example of St Mary the Virgin Church at Nunthorpe, which transformed a "scruffy verge" into a "community wildlife haven". In her report of the project, Jennie Adams brings together a number of significant and inter-related factors:

> *The transformation from the scruffy grass verge, which was littered with fast food packaging and dog mess, to a wildlife garden was miraculous. It all started at a meeting of the green group (the parish ecology group) where we were organising a litter pick for the car park and verge. Feeling that this was not the answer I suggested that we should make a long-term change to the car park as it was an eyesore and also repellent to wildlife.*
>
> *To combat the problems we decided to plant a garden to encourage birds and insects. A parishioner who was taking a garden design course drew up a fantastic plan and a collection of people armed with spades gathered to put the plan into action by initially removing the litter and turf. The project escalated as, due to its content, we had to remove the top layer of soil. Many supported the project with time, plants and money, including Christian Ecology Link who provided a small grant. The planting took two days, aided for one day by pupils from Nunthorpe Primary School. Once the garden was finished signs were made asking people not to walk across it or let their dog foul it.*
>
> *The garden is a tremendous success; not only has it provided a valuable habitat for wildlife but has brought the community together and spread the message that God's environment is important for a younger generation.14*

Eco-mission initiatives also focussed on water, mainly in terms of small and basic items such as monitoring its use, ensuring that leaking taps were fixed, and installing dual flush toilets. Several congregations reported that

---

12 Interview 2007.
13 Interview 2007.
14 EcoCongregation website, England.

they used building materials from sustainable forests. Another prominent category related to the purchase of eco-friendly cleaning products, recycled paper, and the like.

A more fundamental eco-mission program is being undertaken by the Stirling Methodist Church. This congregation is close to the heart of a campaign to make the Riverside area of Stirling the first carbon neutral community in Scotland. The area has a population of approximately 1,500 people, but they plan to attack climate change by lowering their carbon footprint. A Carbon Footprint Survey is being issued with the assistance of Strathclyde University, with the aim of measuring average carbon emissions and proposing measures for reducing them. The initiative now has widespread support in the community, but it began as an initiative of Church members who were committed to being an "eco congregation". Their hope is that others will be encouraged to take up the initiative.

Education

Education programs and workshops have an important role to play, even if at this stage they are not common or widespread. I have previously mentioned the Eco Workshop I conducted at Caloundra, but there have been other examples as well. In addition there is clearly an educational component in informed preaching that picks up the perspective of Earth. There is considerable scope for the expansion of this theme.

In Britain, St John the Evangelist Church at Hurst Green adopted a more direct educational approach through a "Church and Community Environment Day" aimed at raising awareness in and beyond the local Church community. With the help of a Green Partnership Award, the local Energy Efficiency Advice Centre and the Lancashire Wildlife Trust, the Church arranged speakers on energy efficiency, green funerals, greening the Church, spiritual responsibility in today's world, and wildlife conservation in churchyards. Such an exercise, within its unique context, is significant as a model in several ways. It establishes a helpful eco-partnership between the Church and local groups, declares that the Church has a relevant eco agenda, and it educated both the Church and the wider community. It is not surprising that feedback included comments such as "this initiative has provided inspiration for the church and community – it has helped me to gather information to take back to my work at school."

Media Usage

Media publicity is one area that is often not handled with much imagination. Saints Mary and John Church at Oxford have had articles in the local press, while Evesham Methodist had "good coverage in the local press and in national Christian media" after their Eco Award. Eco congregations also frequently report the regular publication of ecologically relevant material in their magazines. One pertinent example is St Chad's at Leeds. In reporting that environmental material is regularly included in the Parish paper, Dalton indicated that the magazine frequently finds its way into the community. She stated, "A lot of people read it who don't go to Church. It has been found in the local laundrette, and read by Asians who are Muslims. I fairly frequently get phone calls from people wanting to know how they can reuse something rather than just landfill it, so I consider that almost as outreach work"[15].

This is one area with under-utilised potential. As a general rule we are not good at identifying newsworthy programs or events, especially those of a good news type. A creative imagination and some professional advice may help Church or religious groups to "sell" their environmental work more effectively.

Personal Lifestyle

The sixth area moves from corporate lifestyle integrity to personal lifestyle issues, and not least the challenge for individual Church members to adopt an eco-friendly personal lifestyle. In my own case, at our previous home my wife and I had a significant native garden on a 777m2 suburban block of land, including flowering trees and shrubs that attract native birdlife. We installed two water tanks of 10,000 litres in all, while green waste that we were not able to compost ourselves was recycled through the Regional Council, and other waste was also recycled, so that our normal weekly landfill waste was reduced to two small bags. In addition we insulated our home, installed a solar hot water system, photovoltaic cells to generate 1.5 kilowatts of electricity, and we drove a small car, so that in all possible ways we have taken steps to reduce our carbon footprint. We would not claim that our response is unique, but rather that it is illustrative of what is possible in a suburban context.

---

15 Interview 2007.

An Integrated Approach

It will be obvious that what I have outlined is illustrative rather than comprehensive. There are very many stories that could be told from the perspective of different countries, and the situation is constantly changing. Nevertheless I have sought to illustrate what is happening and the possibilities for the future in a thematic way that may inspire some imaginative and creative responses. Every situation is different, but what is needed is an integrated plan which helps to ensure that the various dimensions are covered and that there is a balance between local, regional, national and global issues.

The question of balance between local and global issues is one that must be asked of the emerging eco-mission themes. My impression is that many congregations have tended to focus quite strongly on local issues with little obvious reference to the global context. The problem is not in engagement with local issues in a particular community; indeed, such an approach will be inevitable if there is to be meaningful engagement with environmental issues. The global situation involving climate change and other major issues is so large that the best one can hope to do is to grasp "the near edge" of it. Thus, my contention is that eco-mission invariably reflects several contexts simultaneously; if it begins locally, it must also take account of regional, national, and certainly of the global situation.

A holistic approach to eco-mission will, I believe, include elements of all the sectors – worship and education, local community issues, and global issues. Put another way, the planet will not be saved by changing light bulbs, recycling, and cleaning up the Church grounds; but there is hope when such "near edge" items become the means by which people begin to engage more deeply with the core environmental issues.

Eco-Mission Inhibitors

It is inevitable that even with the best of intentions there will be a number of factors working against successful eco-mission outcomes, and it is important that we try to understand some of those inhibitors or blocks. These have been identified from observation of congregations in both England and Australia. I propose to deal with them under three main categories, viz. basic theology and approach to mission, perceptions and feelings, and practical issues.

Theology and Approach to Mission

The first inhibitor relates to a particular type of theology and approach to mission. At a global level, it is clear that some theological ideas represent a significant barrier to eco-mission. I noted earlier that some people reject the idea that Christian mission and theology should have an ecological dimension at all. Without any doubt there are those who believe that the Earth is about to be destroyed in a massive eschatological event, and God will create a new heaven and a new earth. Further, there are those who believe that the Earth is of no consequence, since all that is important is saving the souls of people; the resulting human-centred focus of mission will be obvious enough. I would argue that such views exist largely at an extreme, and that such a militant opposition to eco-theology and eco-mission is probably not a major factor in the average "mainstream" denomination.

The more significant issue is undoubtedly one of a lack of theological awareness or sophistication. In the same vein, and without moving to a theological extreme, it may also be argued that a large part of the problem is that the Church is the inheritor of the overwhelmingly anthropocentric theology and mission practices of centuries. We reflected on that in the previous chapter on mission. In such a context, "nature" was a "given", and the notion of creation care simply did not arise. It is now clear to most people, regardless of their religious orientation, that nature can no longer be taken for granted.

Another basic inhibitor is a residual reservation about the role of science vis-á-vis religious faith, resulting in a demonising of the scientific approach and contribution. But the issue is further clouded by the claims of a small minority of scientists who, like Singer and Avery, seek to persuade the general public that global warming is a natural phenomenon, and the notion of human-induced climate change is false. The fact that Singer and Avery's book *Unstoppable Climate Change* is lauded as a best seller is a concern, and clearly indicates that such a view, however mistaken, cannot be ignored. For more reasons than one, people who do not want to believe the science will quickly find refuge and solace in their prophecy of comfort.

Several other issues may be raised here. A residual Neo-Platonic influence in some Christian theology leads to an aversion to anything of a material nature, and therefore to what I would argue is a limited view of what is spiritual. At a more mundane level, a common approach is the simplistic understanding that the environment is outside the scope of the Church's mission. A variation on the above responses is the perception that inertia is often caused by the fact that people are simply not convinced, that they don't understand what is taking place environmentally, and that they don't know what to think or don't know what to do.

Perceptions and Feelings

The second inhibitor relates to perceptions and feelings. In many respects it may be said that whether or not they reflect reality, feelings are facts. Perceptions and feelings, therefore, even when they are essentially irrational, act as powerful motivators or inhibitors. A range of factors has been identified by my respondents. Because this matter has historically not been strong in the Church's thought and action, and because the environment also is a significant political issue, some people have a real fear of what they regard as green extremism with a political edge, or the perception that any recognition of the importance of nature must be "new age". This is a fear that Campolo[16] identified quite clearly. Other perceptions and fears include the thought that there is nothing that the Church or individuals can do, or that anything that might be attempted would inevitably cost a significant amount of money, both of which I would contend are demonstrably baseless. At a different level is the fear that any action that might be taken would mean changing one's lifestyle; Singer and Avery's work plays on that fear significantly. Here it has to be said that if such a perception is a fear, then it is well founded, in the sense that one of the fundamental messages emerging from the current eco-crisis is that there will be a price to pay if there is to be a future, and the longer we leave it the higher the price will be; as a people we must be prepared to change and to live more simply.

Practical Issues

A range of practical issues may also be recognised as inhibiting factors, beginning with the significant fact that many congregations are small in size and aged in composition. When a congregation is finding it a struggle just to survive, even from an emotional perspective, it is exceedingly difficult to summon the energy or the vision to deal with an issue that seems so

16 Tony Campolo, T. *How to Rescue the Earth Without Worshipping Nature.* (Milton Keynes: Word Publishing, 1992).

remote and removed from the immediate concern. This remains the case even when the congregation has an ecologically-aware leadership.

As an extension of that, a lack of funds must be acknowledged as the second serious inhibiting factor, in that some eco-mission responses do cost money, such as a decision to purchase green power or to install solar PV cells; if funds are short, even with the best intention, the green option may not be open. The Church of the Ascension at Ealing is a case in point. This church was one of the first to trial Eco-Congregation's Eco Award program in England, and it has undertaken a range of eco-mission activity, including regular eco-worship and an environmental audit; the members know what needs to be done. The Rector indicated that they are a small congregation on a "very tight budget". They do what they can; they use energy-efficient light bulbs, and they don't use disposable paper cups. This difficulty is effectively summarised in Reed's observation: "We're not at the moment with a green energy supply for the simple reason that every time we've looked into it, it would cost us money, and we just can't afford to do that. And similarly we can't afford to have a more energy-efficient heating system; we just don't have the 5-figure sum to upgrade that at the moment"[17]. Again, there is no obvious solution to this dilemma, but it is an important inhibitor of eco-mission locally.

A third prominent inhibitor is the pressure of other priorities, creating a situation in which there is simply not the time or energy to devote to an aspect of mission that would require fresh thinking. It is easy to be critical of such a position, but from my own experience I have to say that I can understand the problem only too well. Yet while that difficulty is recognised, it may also be pointed out that by focussing on the environment as a mission issue, it is at least possible that it could be the one issue that connects with the community and helps the congregation to revive itself.

Fourth, and often as a corollary of the first issue, a lack of the necessary leadership or personnel with the necessary expertise and capability of enabling a local eco-mission program can be a significant problem. When practitioners do not have a ready source of expertise, materials, and workable ideas, any potential eco-mission is deferred as simply too hard and inaccessible. In the case of a number of smaller British congregations

---

17 Interview 2007.

I encountered, such as at Derby and at Cleeve, the role of leadership has been taken very effectively by the clergyperson, who has sometimes then been able to draw several others into active involvement. However, a major concern remains when that clergyperson is removed from the situation; clearly, there is no easy answer to this problem.

Fifth, even in situations where leadership should not be overly problematic, eco-mission is simply not part of their consciousness. Because Christian mission has for so long had primarily, if not solely, a human focus, it does not occur to them that there is an issue here. Thus, a lack of vision in local leadership must be recognised as one of the inhibitors of eco-mission.

Sixth, Church governance issues can also be important; the Adelaide Eco-faith community represents a particular case study. In real terms it should be regarded as an experiment. Dr Jason John left after two years and the group continued under its own management, although his statement to me was that it could have worked if there was a will to do so. In such a situation as this a number of factors may contribute to the difficulties, including interpersonal conflicts and ministry team issues, differing attitudes to management, the lack of a clear and agreed vision, an insecure financial base for the project and other factors.

A seventh issue, while not in itself a block to eco-mission, is not especially helpful to it either. My observation is that many congregations with an eco-mission program either do not have a written mission statement or at least one that goes beyond the most elementary level. Without an adequate Statement eco-mission is bound either to struggle, or at least to lack direction. Holy Trinity Church at Skipton, on the other hand, has a concise but helpful eco-mission statement, in which such things as basic goals and lines of responsibility are identified. This gives eco-mission some valuable legitimacy in that congregation, and aids a spirit of intentionality in that mission.

An eighth factor is the general lack of comprehensive eco-theological and eco-mission education of leaders and clergy. Anecdotal evidence suggests that the theological education of prospective clergy is often not strong in this area.

I would have to add one further issue that has often emerged from conversations with a number of people involved in this field, and that is a real sense of isolation. The truth is that there are pockets of eco-mission activity all over Australia, but many of them are operating in isolation from the others, and the resulting feeling of being virtually alone is not conducive to strong and confident activity. However, "isolation" is a relative term that depends in no small measure on the particular context; it certainly varies from one country or region to another. Another possible issue is the perception of a lack of denominational support for eco-mission, and even if that may not always be entirely fair, perceptions matter.

Analysis

Other factors could undoubtedly be added to the list of eco-mission inhibitors indicated above. It is interesting though to compare perceived inhibitors in the Australian situation with perceived blocks in a very different British context. My conclusion is that in spite of those differences the inhibitors are remarkably similar.

This issue is important in that any advance in the field of eco-mission will be against the background of the fears, perceptions, beliefs, and practical problems of many people who are either not currently engaged, or are inadequately engaged in eco-mission, and it must take account of that context. It may be obvious that in many cases there are no quick and easy solutions; but the question that must be asked is how the identified blocks relate to actual eco-mission programs. What are the gaps, and what strategies might help to bridge those gaps in a more positive way?

It is clear that generally speaking Churches need to do more in this area of concern; but when the inhibitors I have identified are set down beside available or potential eco-mission programs and resources, at least some of the gaps are diminished or disappear. The programs that relate specifically to inhibitors may be grouped in several ways. First, a comprehensive program of education will address issues of the background science, together with issues of eco-theology and eco-mission theology, even though educational workshops and seminars cannot on their own deal with attitudes of apathy or closed minds. Second, worship and preaching with an ecological focus will address some of the feelings and perceptions some people may have. Third, encouragement of creation spirituality in the context of green space and native gardens has the possibility of communicating with people at a deep level. Fourth, an expanding network of expertise and support, together with the provision of a range of program ideas will gradually address the difficulty of churches not knowing what to do. The main area of blockage that is not easily addressed by a corresponding program is the shortage of funds, for example to carry out some building-related projects; nor can any program add more hours to the day or roll back the tide of time. But in spite of problems, I contend that people who are seized by an ideal and a vision will find some ways, within their capacity, to begin to be part of the answer rather than part of the problem.

One final aspect may be mentioned, and in saying this I know I am repeating myself. But the lack of a locally-owned Eco-mission Statement will always be a problem, regardless of location. A clearly enunciated vision and specific goals, adopted and owned, will be a strong positive way to the future.

An Ecumenical Approach

I have argued that humankind is part of "the web of life"; that is, we are part of creation, not above and beyond it. In a similar way, it may be argued that Church members are not only part of their particular branch of the Christian Church, but members also of the Church as a whole, and of the wider community beyond the Church. Thus, I found that there was overwhelming support for eco-mission to be exercised on an ecumenical basis. Lowry's response was typical of many: "Ecumenical eco-projects will make a stronger impact on the wider community, and give a broader base on which to work and witness....[18]" Other responses argued that it would offer a more consistent response, provide a better flow of ideas, and that it would provide "a wonderful inclusivity in dealing with a global crisis[19]". But in several cases there was a degree of caution, with respondents thinking that it would be easier to avoid the issue, that an ecumenical approach may result in more talk than action, or that ecumenism takes time.

However, a number of points need to be made. First, it is clear from a range of statements cited earlier that there is already a strong ecumenical approach at work at the highest level of Church administration, as in the case of Councils of Churches or world confessional bodies, and I would contend that this can only be helpful. At the local level, as I have shown, effective eco-mission is almost bound to have its roots in a particular congregation,

18 Interview 2008.
19 Neil Interview 2008.

but that does not mean that it must remain there. My argument is therefore that eco-mission may be both specific and ecumenical at the same time. Second, it is clear from the British experience that the ecumenical approach is strongest and most effective at the level just beyond the congregation, as in the case of EcoCongregation, the A Rocha organisation, and others.

At a wider level, another area in which there was close to unanimity was support for the idea of engaging the political processes on behalf of the environment. Some respondents qualified their affirmation with observations such as any comment should be informed, the Church should be the conscience of the nation, and any views expressed must be balanced. Dawn Wilson's approach was that "saying things are political and none of our business is a 'cop-out' – an excuse for continuing 'as is' while blaming the government.[20]" Dr Chris Walker stated that such engagement with the political process "affirms God's concern for the world and not just humans... The Church needs to speak with its own voice and perspective and avoid being seen as an ill informed lobby group.[21]"

Role of Schools

One area that could have a significant environmental impact as an extension of congregational eco-mission initiatives is that of educational establishments, most notably schools. Clearly this is potentially a very large issue that may be vulnerable to changing Government policies, and therefore it is not possible to pursue it here or to determine what impact the educational system might have in a wider setting. However, it may be noted that research on sustainability education in Tasmanian schools is currently being undertaken. Beyond that, it is worth noting that Catholic Education in Queensland has a well-developed environmental education program with a strong theological and educational underpinning. A report in 2008 indicated that over 32 schools were active environmentally. One example of the broader potential of children to lead the way may suffice. Liza Neil is an environmental architect who has a commitment to Our Lady of the Rosary School, which is a Parish school in Caloundra; her comment was that environmentally the school "is now possibly driving the Parish rather than the other way round". The program is obviously still in the early stages

---

20 Interview 2008.
21 Interview 2008.

of development; but Neil states "We've just had a 'Green' Community Fun Run. We've saved 1.5 tonnes of CO_2 through car-free challenges and the kids are becoming eco-activists and teaching us all". She adds, "I love it when the Grade 3 activists tell the Grade 7's not to litter.[22]"

It is apparent that at this point of time the "eco-activism" of the school has had little impact on the associated congregation. However, when anecdotal evidence is added to the zeal of younger students, it at least gives rise to hope. Moreover, if other state, church, and independent schools had a comparable program, the results in time could be significant.

Structural Issues

It is a common practice to locate environmental issues in the Social Justice section of denominational structures, and it must be acknowledged that there is a certain logic involved in such a link. As I have argued in this book, there is a strong relationship between justice for people and justice for the planet. However, in spite of an assertion that personnel in the different sections of the hierarchy are in regular communication, I contend that the danger of an excessive compartmentalising of issues is very real, and that it becomes evident in a tendency to separate social justice from day-to-day mission in congregations.

I do not propose to attempt a solution to the question of where eco-mission fits in a Church structure, except to say that it needs careful thought. I am not seeking here to point a finger of blame at any individual or organisation, but rather to point towards the limitations of some of our administrative systems. My contention is that the theology which nurtures a social justice conscience and a concern for our environment must also inform the mission of the Church, not just at a national or state level, but locally; and local leaders must be helped to confront and deal with the issues involved. Perhaps a British experience may once again provide at least food for thought. In 2007, Churches Together in Britain and Ireland was overhauling its committee structure. As the General Secretary explained it to me, rather than having a committee for the environment, this was to become part of the brief of every committee. There are dangers there as well because of the human element; my point is that the connections need to be made, and reinforced by appropriate systems of administration.

---

22 Interview 2008.

Such an approach in Britain reflects Conradie's stance that an ecological ethic or ethos carries implications that reach into virtually every aspect of life. Thus, against the background of a widespread perception that eco-mission represents just one more issue the Church is called upon to deal with, Conradie's assertion is important. "There is ... no need to add environmental concerns to an already over-crowded and overwhelming agenda of local churches and ecumenical bodies. Instead, the entire life and praxis of the church should include an ecological dimension and vision[23]". It follows that what is required is a fundamentally different mindset from that which often prevails in the Church, especially at state and local levels.

Eco-Mission Support Systems

One issue of some importance, not least in the diverse Australian context, is the way in which the problem of isolation can be managed and congregations supported in their effort to embrace eco-mission. There are at least two issues here. The first relates to the personal care of people involved in eco-mission, against the background that they are perceptively often operating near the edge of accepted Christian mission, and in many circles their cause is not yet widely accepted. When disappointment is added to feelings of isolation, an energy-sapping despondency may result. In the context of the largely-lapsed Earth Ministry initiative in Sydney, I found myself asking, "Who cares for the carers?" There is no easy answer to this, but the question of the personal and pastoral care of eco-mission practitioners must at least be on the table.

Integrating Eco-Mission

I have sought to show that eco-mission is based on a practical theological approach to eco-theology and some of the most basic Christian doctrines; such a theologically-based approach to eco-mission therefore places it squarely within the mainstream of Christian mission. In other words, an eco-mission theology will rise out of a sound ecological theology, and, I am arguing, will be expressed in terms of a composite stewardship model. How then can an intentional approach to eco-mission be implemented and integrated into the Church's missional practice? In summary I propose an 8-step program to address the basic issues.

---

23 Ernst M Conradie, ed. *Towards an Agenda for Ecological Theology: An Intercontinental Dialogue.* (London: Equinox Publishing, 2005), 282.

First, reflect on the nature and mission of the Church. It is necessary to be clear about the current situation, to identify and determine to address any problem areas or issues relating to mission. There will always be a problem when the Church at whatever level has not grasped the theological imperative for creation care, when it becomes confused by the often-phoney debate about whether climate change, for example, is real, or when human greed or a simple need to survive combine with a narrow definition of "economy" to render sustainability as secondary to financial considerations.

Problems will always occur when the Church is effectively viewed as a club, in which case mission, however it is defined, will be in trouble. When mission is not intentional but is seized by lethargy, there is a need to go right back to the basics to rediscover what faith and church are all about. Similarly, I suspect that some of us have effectively not moved past what Habel describes as the 1st mission of the Church.

Second, the existence of environmental policy statements at both an ecumenical level and at a National-State denominational level is a significant factor, since they reflect a high degree of consensus. Such Statements potentially provide a fundamental direction and a sense of cohesion in this matter. The operative word here is "potentially", since it becomes clear that such statements do not always filter through to the local level.

That leads to a third step, namely the ownership of an ecological mission policy at a congregation or Parish level. Without that, finely worded environmental statements tend to dissipate or simply gather dust in ecclesiastical archives, and that has happened all too often! Such an "ownership" of eco-mission may be applied in several ways.

At a basic level, the congregation needs to affirm a general policy, a *modus operandi* that is built upon sustainable and Earth-friendly values. This may be regarded as a statement of fundamental principles upon which specific goals will be based. Effective environmental action can only be based on the conviction that eco-theology and eco-mission are not an optional extra but are part of the Gospel itself. At every level of the Church, and not least in congregational terms where there are often many competing options, what that means in the first instance is the adoption of an eco-mission vision statement.

But it will clearly be important for the local church to establish clear and specific eco-mission goals at periodic intervals. In keeping with the development of a mission strategy in other areas, eco-mission goals will need to be what is sometimes captured by the acronym SMARTER; that is, they will need to be specific, measurable, achievable, realistic, timed, evaluated, and revised. A local eco-mission group does not have to be large in order to be effective, but such a group needs to take the lead in identifying clear eco-mission goals, and thus in encouraging their congregation to become involved. Such an approach is used quite consistently in Britain, where congregations associated with the EcoCongregation organization have succeeded in achieving a wide range of environmental outcomes, with of course a greatly enhanced awareness on the part of congregation members.

Fourth, because of the long silence on this subject over the years, the church will need to consider programs of environmental and eco-theological education. Once again, this will need to be conceived and applied at a number of levels. State and national jurisdictions will have a role to play. In a sense they will need to build on fundamental policy statements in specific ways to ensure that eco-theological or eco-mission issues remain an essential part of the church's awareness. This would be applied, for example, in the work of mission consultants, in public statements, group studies, and in other ways.

Theological educators have a particular role in this process as they prepare men and women for ordination. Unless the basic elements of eco-theology and eco-mission are included in the curriculum, an essentially anthropocentric approach to mission will continue to dominate. My point is that one cannot adequately study basic doctrines such as creation, incarnation, and grace without including the wider perspective of the Earth. Nor can one study the theology and practice of mission without including the fundamentals of eco-mission. More than that, in keeping with other aspects of Christian mission, a constantly changing social context will require a measure of in-service training or continuing education for existing clergy if they are to be able to assist their congregations to become change agents in a matter that grows more acute on an almost daily basis. Finally, it need hardly be said that the process of eco-theological education needs to filter through to the level of the local congregation, to those who in fact become the "foot soldiers" of the churches' eco-mission.

Fifth, an eco-theological awareness will need to extend to the worship life and spirituality of the church. In a sense it may almost be argued that this is already starting to happen, although it is still the exception. It is clear that there is a plethora of environmental worship resources available; a web search for "worship resources environment" inevitably results in a great many listings from various parts of the world! Even though some of the material may need to be adapted for a particular national or regional context, busy Parish clergy have access to a great deal of fine material, thus enabling them to construct helpful liturgies. However, it is arguable that in many instances ecologically-based worship remains largely a fringe activity, and that worship reflecting an Earth-awareness is not common at the local level. Harvest festivals, loved so dearly by a former generation, and World Environment Day each June, are just two examples of annual occasions when such worship would be particularly appropriate.

Sixth, eco-theological implications for Christian mission must resonate with a personal and corporate lifestyle that is consistent with those principles. A good deal of readily accessible material has been produced on this subject, loosely based on the maxim "reduce, reuse, recycle". Thus, a whole range of practical measures are included, ranging from the use of solar hot water, the installation of a rainwater tank, a more eco-friendly motor vehicle, and a great deal more. At one level this may not seem very significant, but very importantly it represents a personal commitment, and if multiplied across the population it is no small matter. I will consider practical responses in more detail in Chapter 7.

Seventh, there is an on-going need to deal with structural issues in terms of where eco-mission fits in the overall program (including budgets!) of the Church. This is not an easy matter, but there needs to be a balance between various elements. There is a need for specific expertise to assist the Church in this important aspect of its life. But consciousness of creation care must relate to the whole of our life together, whether it is in the way Synod meetings are conducted, mission consultations are structured, our use of resources or anything else.

Eighth, the significance of ecumenical and interfaith issues can hardly be over-stated in terms of eco-mission. If we were prepared to explore ways in which other parts of the Church relate to this issue we might find that insights come from what may be for us unexpected sources, such as the Orthodox Church. But the Anglican Church's widely acclaimed "Five Marks of Mission" may be regarded as particularly significant, and other parts of the wider church would do well to consider their formal adoption. The fifth "mark of mission" specifically names creation care as part of our mission.

Conclusion

In this chapter I have sought to show something of the shape and context of eco-mission in Australian churches, including a dimension of what we might learn from overseas sources. As I have previously indicated, this is indicative and illustrative rather than comprehensive. It begins within an international and ecumenical background which is shaped to some extent by pronouncements and resolutions at a national level. But the essential practical outcomes invariably emerge at a local level, with some direction and support from state and regional jurisdictions. Thus, I have considered a range of factors that might either encourage or inhibit effective eco-mission. This has included matters regarding underlying attitudes, some ways in which eco-mission might begin, the place of mission statements, and a number of general themes by which eco-mission programs might be summarised. Other important dimensions relate to the need for adequate support systems, including some structural issues, and the potential for productive international dialogue.

In the final chapter I will summarise the conclusions we might draw from our study and seek to give an indication of what an Australian eco church might look like.

CHAPTER EIGHT

Conclusion: A Future with Hope

I have previously cited Moltmann to the effect that the "ecological crisis" is in reality "a crisis of the whole life system of the modern industrial world"[1]. Conradie would agree, arguing that the crisis is primarily cultural rather than ecological. He suggests that "what is required is a fundamental change of orientation, a *metanoia*"[2]. That is true both for the Church as a whole and for the individuals who are part of it.

But have we gone too far? The overwhelming message of climate science is that it is already too late to avoid permanent damage to the global environment which will have serious consequences for life on Earth; put another way we are either heading for the cliff with our foot on the throttle or we are already over the cliff. Is it possible to have a future with hope in spite of the bad news, or shall we give way to despair? This is an important issue; but there is a prior theological question.

The Way of Hope

Part of the eco-theology debate centres around the question of what constitutes the crown of creation. Some may answer that it is of course humankind, or in some cases even *man*kind! I believe that Moltmann is right in his perhaps surprising answer that it is in fact the Sabbath. In looking back to the Genesis 1 account of creation von Rad makes the point that while history situates in the sixth day, the Sabbath represents the future. We find ourselves at the point where the sixth day meets the seventh day; but however much we might wish we had done something differently, we cannot go back. We can only go forwards into the seventh day which is the future. Yet it is true that our lives continue to be shaped by the past.

Can we find the way of hope and so avoid the alternative of despair? There is a famous painting by George Frederic Watts called "Hope". It depicts a female figure sitting blindfolded and hunched on a globe, clutching a lyre with only one string intact. Her head is close to the instrument, perhaps so

---

1 Moltmann, *God in Creation*, 23.
2 Conradie, ed. *Towards an Agenda*, 285.

she might hear whatever sound she could make with the sole remaining string. The question both now and then is how this depiction might be understood. According to Watts, "Hope need not mean expectancy. It suggests here rather the music which can come from the remaining chord"[3]. Watts' melancholy depiction of hope was criticised; G.K. Chesterton for example suggested that a better title would be *Despair*. The message from this thought-provoking painting is that the difference between hope and despair may largely be in the way we view a situation.

It is important to emphasize here that hope is not blind. It is not some kind of unrealistic fantasy. Rather I suggest that while hope in the Biblical sense has its eyes wide open and is able to see a situation as it really is, it is also able to see beyond the immediate scene to something more from God. Several Biblical images are relevant here.

In the book of Jeremiah the prophet addresses the situation of a people facing exile and who are understandably finding that difficult. Two contrasting approaches are presented. First, Jeremiah has a battle with false prophets who "… keep saying to those who despise the word of the Lord, 'It shall be well with you'; and to all who stubbornly follow their own stubborn hearts, they say, 'No calamity shall come upon you'"[4]. Hope does not spring from a Pollyanna-like conviction that all is well, but rather from a capacity to look at reality and begin to deal with it. Second, Jeremiah's counsel is to have a positive attitude to life in exile in Babylon. In Chapter 29 he speaks of building and planting, of seeking the welfare of the city in which they find themselves. "For surely I know the plans I have for you, says the Lord, plans for your welfare and not for harm, to give you a future with hope"[5].

A second image is also worth pondering, and that is in Hosea 2 verse 15 in which God declares through the prophet that the Valley of Achor would be "a door of hope". The point is that the Valley of Achor was a place of human sin on the journey into the Promised Land; but that is precisely where hope is to be found. The sin we are talking about now is not the theft of some silver, but the despoiling of creation; it is in turning to face that reality that hope is still to be found.

---

3 En.wikipedia.org/wiki/Hope accessed Aug 2013.
4 Jeremiah 23:17
5 Jeremiah 29:11

The promise of God is expressed in 1st Peter as "new birth into a living hope"[6], and while that is a gift from God, in environmental terms at least it does not fall ready-made from the sky. Harry Emerson Fosdick once reflected that "We are often waiting for God to do for us what God is waiting to do through us". That is very apt in the current situation; we need to work together with God. In a situation that you would not have chosen, don't resort to despair or denial; rather build a future according to God's design.

In Chapter 4 we dealt with that troublesome passage in 2nd Peter 3, and found that apparent cosmic destruction by God is in reality about the renewal of the Earth; it is not that the earth "will be burned up", but that "the earth and everything that is done on it will be disclosed." In the meantime, as 2nd Peter goes on to declare, "... we wait for new heavens and a new earth, where righteousness is at home"[7]. That too is a reflection of the apocalyptic Revelation to John of "a new heaven and a new earth"; what is on offer here is a blessing, not a curse. It is the vision of an ultimately renewed Earth.

In any event, the Sabbath concept includes the reaffirmation of a sense of covenant between God, humanity, and creation; and for Deane-Drummond it implies a sense of dependence, of wonder, and of deep joy in creation in all its variety. She also urges that we learn to *love* creation as a gift of God's love, and that when faith is able to glimpse the glory of God, it leads to a context of love, wonder, humility, and wisdom in which environmental decision-making becomes truly possible. Thus it is essential to find ways to balance the sense of creation as gift with the competing demands of ecological justice. Deane-Drummond is reflecting Moltmann when she states, "I suggest that living from the Sabbath leads to transformation, a transformation of encounter, a renewal of covenant, which we can rightly name as a *cosmic covenant....*"[8].

Looking back, looking forward

What I have sought to do in this book is to argue from a theological and biblical perspective for the inclusion of ecological mission as an important aspect of the mission of the Church. As such, I am arguing that it is not a side issue or an optional extra, but part of the mainstream of that mission.

---

6 1st Peter 1:3

7 2nd Peter 3:13.

8 Celia Deane-Drummond, *The Ethics of Nature.* (Malden, MA: Blackwell Publications. 2004), 11.

In doing this, my aim has been to establish a connection between theology in general, a theology of Christian mission, and the exercise of that mission in practical terms; thus, each chapter has built upon the previous one. I contend that it is imperative for the practitioner at all levels to grasp such a connection as integral to the Christian faith.

A number of points may be made briefly. First, the practice of Christian mission needs to be far more than a mere pragmatic response to the circumstances in which Church communities find themselves; even though that existential context will obviously be important, the mission itself must emerge out of a theological context. Second, in following a practical theology paradigm, I take it as a methodological "given" that theory and praxis will interact in terms of the "hermeneutic spiral" to which I made reference in chapter 2, rather than the praxis being the mere outworking of a predetermined theory.

Thus, within the context of both a global and an Australian eco-crisis, I have sought to argue the case for a credible eco-theology; however, I have argued that such a practical theology is not reactive in nature and does not need a physical crisis to justify a response, since in Christian biblical and theological terms it is rooted in the call of God to care for creation. Once the validity of what I have termed an eco-friendly approach to theology is acknowledged, it is possible to explore the more practical aspects of that theology. In the light of this study I believe that a model for an eco-church in Australia starts to take shape.

Theological Implications

There are several principal and related implications for Christian theology and ecclesiastical practice. In the background there may be the recognition that at times there has been a theological crisis alongside the environmental one, at least at a grassroots level. Thus, when a theology of Christian mission is added to a theology of creation, or eco-theology, what emerges is a second aspect of a crisis, but this time it is spiritual and theological in nature, expressed in the widespread failure of the Church to grasp the significance of the natural environment, or God's creation, in its approach to mission. Put another way, this would be the confession that for a very long time Christians and Churches have generally failed to grasp the environmental or creation-care theological implications that in one form or another have always been present.

What this suggests is that in the first instance there is a need to re-think the assumptions we bring to a reading of Scripture and our understanding of reality. The dominant hermeneutical assumption has been, and in many respects remains, human-focussed. Habel's advocacy of a hermeneutic of suspicion, to which I made reference in chapter 2, is, in my view, pertinent. When the hermeneutical perspective shifts from a human to an earth focus, new understandings become possible. Habel's "Earth Bible"[9] series is an example of that; Leal's[10] treatment of some parables of Jesus is another.

Second, it suggests the need to recognise the validity and implications of a theology of creation as it relates to ecological issues. Santmire's categorisation of the Church's historic approach to the place of ecology in the history of theology as ambiguous (chapter 4) may be acknowledged readily; and while that means an anthropocentric theology goes back to the beginning of the Christian faith, it indicates equally that a nature-inclusive approach also has its roots in that same period. But beyond that, I contend that the biblical exegesis and theological reflection on the care of creation has validity in its own right, that it is part of the theological mainstream, and therefore ought not to be overlooked by practitioners but recognised in the Church at large.

Implications for Theory and Ecclesial Practice

Once the theological implications have been established, a range of theoretical implications inevitably ensue. The following list is not necessarily complete, but is indicative of some of the more significant aspects.

First, it is clearly not enough for Churches to make pronouncements about environmental issues, or to simply state what they believe governments should be doing, although that is an important element and it is right that they should do so. Indeed, it is almost inevitable that at a national level at least, the focus will be in that area. However, the Christian community also has an obligation, even a divine calling, to set its own house in order, and to engage in practical eco-mission along with other groups with a related

---

9 Habel, *Readings*
10 Robert Barry Leal, *Through Ecological Eyes: Reflections on Christianity's Environmental Credentials.* (Strathfield NSW: St Paul's Publications, 2006).

vision. I have suggested a number of ways in which that can happen. The widespread community recognition of an eco-crisis presents a powerful opportunity for a practical public theology, or for what might be termed "mission in the public square".

Second, I contend that there are implications for theological education, in the training of clergy and lay leaders. The overwhelming perception of respondents in my research, both in Britain and in Australia, is that eco-theology and its implications is not a high priority. It will be obvious of course that there are a great many pressures on the curricula of theological colleges, and it may not be possible to cover all the ground that may be desirable. It should also be acknowledged that specialised courses such as "the Greening of Mission" at Redcliffe College in England or eco-theology at the United Theological College in New South Wales may occasionally be found, although they do not appear to be common. Nevertheless, even with those acknowledgments, eco-theology and the corresponding mission is still in most cases on the periphery rather than acknowledged as part of the mainstream. I contend that it is not necessary to consume vast amounts of limited time in order to include an eco theme, but rather that the rudiments at least should be included in the core teaching. Thus, for example, it should be acknowledged that a credible approach to teaching a doctrine of God in creation must include an element of caring for creation.

At a more local level, many leaders and congregation members can be reached through workshops and seminars that may take no more than several hours. This has been demonstrated in a number of places including south-east Queensland.

Third, and as an extension of the previous point, programs of continuing education for ministry could very easily add eco-theology and eco-mission as options, especially at a time in which environmental issues are becoming more prominent, more open to change, and in which people with appropriate expertise are becoming available.

Fourth, there are eco-theological implications for denominational structures. As I have suggested in the previous chapters, while eco-mission is clearly related to the area of social justice, it is equally clearly related as a core component of mission. It may be that in the eyes of many, advocating social justice is not fully recognised as authentic and essential core mission either, in which case eco-mission has an even harder task in being recognised. Structures, and therefore boundaries, are both important and inevitable, but I contend that it is also important that structures do not unnecessarily impede the possibilities of eco-mission.

Fifth, it has become apparent from my research that a pervasive sense of eco-mission trying to happen in isolation presents a significant obstacle to effective action, especially when that is combined with significant distances. Against that background, the British Anglican practice of appointing honorary consultants in every diocese or regional area has much to commend it. While it may not be possible to create such a support network overnight, one clear implication is that churches, perhaps acting ecumenically, should address the need to reduce the perception of isolation and to increase the availability of resources and personal support in this mission. A corollary of that is the need to identify appropriately qualified people, regardless of denomination or indeed religion for that matter, so that their expertise may be accessed according to need and their availability.

Sixth, the need for appropriate political engagement was almost unanimously supported by my respondents in Australia. This can happen at all levels, from national, denominational or ecumenical press statements, to the writing of letters to members of parliament, right through to our own face-to-face engagement with our State or Federal members of Parliament. We need the spirit of the prophets!

Seventh, the need to find the right balance between local and global is implicit in the research. At a local level it is inevitable and appropriate that local issues will dominate; but from what I have said above, it is also imperative that local action and insight is ultimately understood in a global context.

Other implications may also be drawn, and will certainly emerge from time to time in the light of further reflection and practice.

An Eco-Church Model for Australia?

There are several concluding questions that may reasonably be asked. For example, are there reasonable grounds for hope that the Christian Church will enhance its effectiveness in eco-mission in the near term, and in cooperation with other concerned agencies and groups? One cannot predict the future, but certainly there is some ground for hope. But if a change in mindset is coming, our prayer might be that it will come soon!

That would appear to be supported by the steady increase in the number of congregations taking the first tentative steps, not only in the direction of a more sustainable future, but also towards a more holistic response to the requirements of Christian mission in the 21st century.

A second and related question might be to ask if it is possible to create a picture of an eco-church model for Australia. The answer must be both yes and no. As eco congregations begin to emerge all over the country, they do so in a great variety of different local contexts, and therefore are to some extent shaped by those factors. Thus, eco congregations are bound to differ in some ways. At the same time, there are many common elements, even across national and hemispherical differences. It may therefore be possible to develop a type of eco-mission template that is sufficiently basic but also cognisant of practical detail in such a way that it may be adapted and adopted by churches existing in radically different circumstances.

It is not my purpose here to attempt to construct such a template, but in addition to the implications noted above, and by way of summary, the following is an example of what such a template may include.

First, I propose that a good starting point for eco-mission may be the identification of some appropriate resources and resource people. This will help to overcome isolation, and ensure that new groups will be able to build on the endeavours of previous groups, and to learn from their mistakes, without the unnecessary need to "reinvent the wheel." A further aspect of that will be the identification of a small core group that will be essential for encouraging the congregation as a whole to become involved in this endeavour.

Second, the pronouncements of global and national ecumenical and denominational bodies will form a significant backdrop and means of intellectual and spiritual support for local practitioners setting out on an eco-mission venture. As I have noted previously, many of those statements and resolutions are strong, and reflect a global Christian consensus on this matter. Local groups may be well advised not to deprive themselves of this means of support. This will also help to ensure that local responses are offered within the context of a global crisis.

Third, the use of educational workshops and other teaching opportunities, including sermons, will help to ensure that any practical activity is soundly based in at least two ways. It will encourage a response that is theologically based and not merely the outworking of pragmatism. But it will also be important to help people understand what is happening to the global environment, while at the same time bearing in mind that the situation is a developing one, and fresh information is constantly coming to hand. In that regard, a resource such as Al Gore's "An Inconvenient Truth" has often proved to be a useful teaching tool.

Fourth, I believe that it is essential that the wider Church create a resource pack such as that prepared by David Pickering for use by the EcoCongregation organisation in Britain. This would provide emerging local groups with a means of determining where they are currently situated environmentally, and also a package of basic resources with a series of issues they can work through. I am also favourably disposed to the idea of relating this material to an award system, on the basis that this provides a structure and a public recognition of stages that have been achieved, and may be used as a further publicity and educative tool.

Fifth, I would assert that it is highly desirable that one of the first steps to be taken in establishing eco-mission locally should be the working through and adoption of an eco-mission statement that sets out the primary vision and aims of the mission. This serves to clarify what the group hopes to achieve, and therefore to be the immediate foundation on which specific goals might be based.

Sixth, a local eco-mission church would need to establish its own priorities and goals, but the template may include a series of project or program options, which while not exhaustive, may nevertheless be a list from which selections may be made; it may also stimulate fresh thinking based on local circumstances or perceptions of the global situation.

Limitations and Additional Issues

It will be obvious that eco-theology and the related theology of eco-mission opens up a very large subject area with the potential to explore numerous aspects at greater depth, but the scope of the fundamental issue is especially apparent when it is applied in terms of a practical theology. Thus, the research involved in this book is necessarily limited to particular aspects of the whole. This work is necessarily incomplete, if only because the picture is changing on a daily basis. What I have sought to do therefore is to clarify the basic theology involved, and to take a snapshot as it were of practical eco-mission at a particular point in time. It is therefore indicative rather than comprehensive.

Other limitations stem from the fact that out of necessity my work has not covered the full range of Christian traditions or denominations. However, in that the focus has been on the main areas of activity, such a limitation is unlikely to be problematic. In addition there are many potential contextual variations around Australia, and while it is important that such a fact should be recognised, it is not possible to explore those variations in any detail. The fact that some people will not be open to a theological argument for Christian eco-mission should at least be noted.

The implications of eco-theology for Christian mission can readily be extended to a number of additional related areas. First, people living in rural communities, and either directly or indirectly deriving their livelihood from the land, face particular issues that deserve attention. Many people on the land are involved in various forms of land care, often in very difficult circumstances. They might be regarded as being on the "front line", with prolonged drought caused by climate change adding a sense of urgency and difficulty to the need to try to survive. These problems are often exacerbated by issues relating to the attempted mix of agriculture and mining.

Second, an eco-theological perspective on the place of the economy and technology would be useful. A popular myth has been that one must choose between the environment and economic progress, but many positive models have begun to emerge. Further research could help to establish an approach to the future that is both affordable and sustainable.

Third, there are the possibilities of inter-faith cooperation, an example of which is the Faith Ecology Network in Australia or Australian Religious Response to Climate Change. Potentially this has many positive implications. I have previously indicated that there is substantial inter-faith agreement concerning the care of the environment, so that a focus on preserving the planet could go a long way towards bridging the gap between followers of major world religions.

Fourth, eco-mission may be viewed as an extension of pastoral care. Graham uses the notion of shalom as a way of exploring lovelessness and injustice, and writes of "harmonizing contention through a ministry of care"[11]. For him, shalom is intended to generate love, justice, and harmony both within and between people, but also with the natural order. He notes that "the ministry of care does not normally directly promote ecological partnership", and that there are ways in which it has a certain "add-on quality"[12]. Thus, Graham believes that a ministry of care must extend to the earth itself, and that "the pastoral caretaker has a responsibility to help persons and families examine their life-style in terms of its ecological consequences, as well as its possibilities for increasing neighbour-love and promoting justice"[13]. Given the fact that pastoral care is rightly perceived as basic to a Church's mission, Graham's holistic approach that effectively extends care beyond people to include the earth is one that could offer some positive possibilities. But relatively little work has been done in this area, and so it may offer an interesting field of further research.

Fifth, there are without doubt many inherent contradictions in modern living. There are some rare individuals who seem to be able to create a sustainable lifestyle, to reduce waste and their carbon footprint to an almost negligible level. But for most people, even those who are environmentally aware, simply living in the modern world can have a high price tag, both economically and in other ways. Thus, in order to advance my research in eco-mission, I needed to fly to the UK, and while an additional payment for carbon credits may appease one's conscience, it does not necessarily pay the environmental cost. How does an individual or a community strike a balance? Is such a balance possible, and what might it look like? This is an area of further deep thought.

Sixth, one aspect of an environmental awakening in recent years has been some significant work being done by dedicated people in schools. One prime example is the Australian Sustainable Schools Initiative, which is promoted by the Federal Government in partnership with the States and Territories. A second example is the work being done through Catholic Education in Queensland. As initiatives such as these tend to increase, what impact might that have, not only on the students as future responsible citizens, but also in a more immediate sense on parents and the wider community? Anecdotal evidence would suggest that children have the capacity to influence their

11 Larry K Graham, *Care of Persons, Care of Worlds: a Psychosystems Approach to Pastoral Care and Counseling.* (Nashville: Abingdon Press, 1992), 159.
12 Graham, *Care of Persons*, 175.
13 Graham, *Care of Persons*, 176.

parents, to share their own environmental education with them. But further research is needed into the role and significance of educational establishments in helping to generate a sustainable future.

Concluding Note

It may well be argued that a range of additional resources is needed if eco-mission is to be as widespread and effective as it needs to be. In speaking with Dr David Pitman, then Moderator of the Queensland Synod of the Uniting Church, I raised the question of finding adequate resources to mount an effective program. His response was that "within what presently exists there is absolutely nothing to prevent a focus on this issue"[14]. I have no doubt that Pitman was right, and even more that his observation is equally applicable across the whole of the Church.

I have argued that some appropriate structures and resources are needed if eco-mission is to take its rightful place in the *missio Dei* exercised through the Church; but in the first instance this is not about structures, governance, or finance, but about commitment to a divine vision for the Earth and all Earth's creatures as God's creation. We can and must do the theology, and wrestle with the theology and practice of mission in a difficult age; but it is more even than that. In the end I believe that it demonstrates the urgent need for a fundamental change of heart and mind, of perception and attitude. It is about rediscovering the passion at the heart of faith and mission, so that as we recognise the presence of God in the natural world we will learn to love creation as God's gift; and when that starts to happen, eco-mission or Earthcare will no longer be a duty but the source of a great joy.

That leads me back to where I began, when I dedicated this book to my grandchildren, for in addition to the ecological, theological and missional case that I have argued, this is also a deeply personal journey. Both they and generations as yet unborn have a reasonable expectation that they will inherit a world fit for them, and it is no less than they deserve. We simply cannot afford to continue living as if there is no tomorrow!

My hope is that while this book cannot of itself create that needed change, it may at least be able to provide sound information to support the change, and encourage an effective approach to Christian ecological mission within the Australian context.

---

14 Interview 2008.

Eco-Mission Checklist – 20 Steps to the Future

The purpose of this Checklist is simply to assist the reader to identify some of the key ingredients of a viable eco-mission program. You may well wish to add to or alter the list; every situation is unique in its own way, but the resources in this book are designed to enable an effective response.

Step 1:

How motivated are you to begin an eco-mission adventure?

Step 2:

Reflect on your experience of God in the natural world.

Step 3:

What theological or other assumptions might you need to question?

Step 4:

Try to come to grips with at least the main parameters of the global environmental situation.

Step 5:

Familiarise yourself with the theological basis of Earthcare.

Step 6:

Reflect on the practical theological base of eco-mission as part of the overall mission of the Church.

Step 7

How sustainable is your personal lifestyle? What changes do you need to make?

Step 8:

Arrange for an environmental audit of your Church.

Step 9:

Identify any resources or resource people available to you.

Step 10:

Identify any other interested people in your Church or community; form an eco-mission group.

Step 11:

Identify any ecumenical or interfaith possibilities for Earthcare.

Step 12:

Arrange to have an eco-theology and mission seminar, and invite other Churches to be involved.

Step 13:

Encourage your Church to include the environment in worship through resources such as Season of Creation.

Step 14:

Explore possibilities for special days such as World Environment Day.

Step 15:

Frame an Eco-Mission Vision Statement for adoption by your Church.

Step 16:

Establish and monitor the implementation of eco-mission goals.

Step17:

What sustainability measures are possible for your Church, such as solar power, water capture and re-use, energy saving practices, or garden composting?

Step 18:

What steps might be taken in terms of a prophetic ministry, such as political pressure on behalf of the environment?

Step 19:

What steps might you consider to support your eco-mission group?

Step 20:

Practice environmental spirituality; experience the presence of God in the natural world.

Select Bibliography

Agard, John et al. *Global Environment Outlook Geo4: environment for development.* New York and Nairobi, Kenya: United Nations Environment Programme, 2007.

Anderson, Ray S. *The Shape of Practical Theology: Empowering Ministry with Theological Praxis.* Downers Grove, Illinois: InterVarsity Press, 2001.

Anglican General Synod. *Green by Grace.* Report, 2004.

Attfield, Robin. 2003. *Environmental Ethics: an Overview for the Twenty-First Century.* Cambridge: Polity Press, 2003.

Attfield R and Dell K eds. *Values, Conflict, and the Environmental Movement.* Second edition, Aldershot; Brookfield, USA: Ashgate, 1996.

Avis, Paul D L. *A Ministry Shaped by Mission.* London and New York: T & T Clark, 2005.

Avis, Paul D L. *Church Drawing Near – Spirituality and Mission in a Post-Christian Culture.* London: T & T Clark, 2003.

Ayre, Clive W. *Climate Change and a Climate of Change in the Church*, in Elvey, Anne and Gormley-O'Brien, David (eds). "Climate Change Cultural Change: Religious Responses and Responsibilities". Preston Vic: Mosaic Press. 2013.

Ayre, Clive W. *Divine Grace and Creation Care*, in Sean Winter (ed.), "Immense, Unfathomed, Unconfined": The Grace of God in Creation, Church and Community: Essays in Honour of Norman Young". Melbourne: Uniting Academic Press, 2013.

Bakken, Peter W, Engel, Joan Gibb, & Engel, J Ronald. *Ecology, Justice, and Christian Faith: a Critical Guide to the Literature.* Westport Conn., and London: Greenwood Press, 1995.

Ball, Ian. *The Earth Beneath: a Crucial Guide to Green Theology.* London: SPCK, 1992.

Bassett, Libby ed. *Earth and Faith: a book of reflection for action.* New York: The United Nations Environment Programme, 2000.

Bauckham, Richard. *Stewardship and Relationship.* In Berry, R.J. ed. "The Care of Creation: Focusing Concern and Action". Leicester: Inter-Varsity Press, 2000.

Beisner, E Calvin. *Where Garden Meets Wilderness: Evangelical Entry into the Environmental Debate.* Grand Rapids, Michigan: Wm B Eerdmans Publishing Co Ltd. (Acton Institute), 1997.

Bergant, Dianne. *The Earth is the Lord's: the Bible, ecology, and worship.* Collegeville, Minn: Liturgical Press, 1998.

Berry, R J. *Christianity and the Environment: Escapist Mysticism or Responsible Stewardship?* In "Science and Christian Belief", 3:3-18, 1991.

Berry, R J ed. *Environmental Stewardship: Critical Perspectives – Past and Present.* London and New York: T & T Clark International, 2006.

Berry, R J. *God's Book of Works: The Nature and Theology of Nature.* London & New York: T & T Clark, 2003.

Berry, R J ed. *The Care of Creation: Focusing Concern and Action.* Leicester: Inter-Varsity Press, 2000.

Berry, Thomas. *The Dream of the Earth.* San Francisco: Sierra Club Books, 1998.

Berry, Thomas and Clark, Thomas. 1991. *Befriending the Earth: A Theology of Reconciliation Between Humans and the Earth.* 23rd Publications, 1991.

Best, Thomas F. 1993. *Koinonia and Justice, Peace, and Creation.* Geneva: World Council of Churches, 1993.

Bevans, Stephen B. 1992. *Models of Contextual Theology: Faith and Cultures.* Maryknoll: Orbis Books, 1992.

Bevans, Stephen B and Schroeder, Roger P. 2005. *Constants in Context: A Theology of Mission for Today.* Maryknoll, New York: Orbis Books, 2005.

Birch Charles, Eakin William, & McDaniel Jay B eds. *Liberating Life: Contemporary Approaches to Ecological Theology.* Maryknoll, NY: Orbis Books, 1990.

Boff, L. 1995. *Ecology and Liberation: a New Paradigm.* Maryknoll, NY: Orbis Books, 1995.

Borg, Marcus J. *The Heart of Christianity.* San Francisco: HarperCollins, 2003.

Borg, Marcus J. *The God we Never Knew.* San Francisco: HarperCollins, 1997.

Bosch, David J. *Believing in the Future: Towards a Missiology of Western Culture.* Valley Forge, Penn.: Trinity Press International, 1995.

Bosch, David J. *Transforming Mission: Paradigm Shifts in Theology of Mission.* Maryknoll, NY: Orbis Books, 1991.

Bosch, David J. *Mission and Ecology.* Missionalia, p97-167, 19 Ag 1991.

Bosch, David J. *Reflections on Biblical Models of Mission.* In Phillips, James M. and Coote, Robert T. eds. *Towards the Twenty-first Century in Christian Mission.* Grand Rapids, MI: Eerdmans, 1993.

Bouma-Prediger, Steven: *The Greening of Theology: The Ecological Models of Rosemary Radford Ruether, Joseph Sittler, and Jurgen Moltmann.* Atlanta Georgia, Scholars Press, 1995.

Bouma-Prediger, Steven. *For the Beauty of the Earth: a Christian Vision for Creation Care.* Grand Rapids, MI: Baker Academic, 2001.

Bradley, Ian. *God is Green: Ecology for Christians.* New York, NY: Doubleday, 1992.

Breuilly, Elizabeth, and Palmer, Martin eds. *Christianity and Ecology.* London: Cassell, 1992.

Bria, Ion ed. *Go Forth in Peace: Orthodox Perspectives on Mission.* Geneva: World Council of Churches, 1986.

Browning, Don S. *A Fundamental Practical Theology: Descriptive and Strategic Proposals.* Minneapolis: Fortress Press, 1996.

Browning, Don S ed. *Practical Theology* San Francisco: Harper & Row, 1983.

Bühlmann, Walbert. *The Chosen Peoples.* Middlegreen, Slough, UK: St Paul Publications, 1982.

Campolo, T. *How to Rescue the Earth Without Worshipping Nature.* Milton Keynes: Word Publishing, 1992.

Cardoza-Orlandi, Carlos F. *Mission: an Essential Guide.* Nashville: Abingdon: Press, 2002.

Carmody, John. *Ecology and Religion: Toward a New Christian Theology of Nature.* New York: Paulist Press, 1983.

Clobus, Rob. *Environmental Care: A Possible Way To Restore God's Image to the Earth.* Eldoret, Kenya: AMECEA Gaba Publications, 1992.

Cobb, John B. *Is it too Late? A Theology of Ecology.* Denton Texas: Environmental Ethics Books, Revised edition, 1995.

Cobb, John B. *Sustainability: Economics, Ecology, and Justice.* Maryknoll, New York: Orbis Books, 1992.

Collins, Paul. *God's Earth: Religion as if Matter Really Mattered.* North Blackburn, Vic: Dove (HarperCollins), 1995.

Conradie, Ernst M ed. *Towards an Agenda for Ecological Theology: An Intercontinental Dialogue.* London: Equinox Publishing, 2005.

Cooper, T. *Green Christianity: Caring for the Whole Creation.* London: Hodder and Stoughton (Spire), 1990.

Crosby, Donald A and Hardwick, Charley D eds. *Religious Experience and Ecological Responsibility.* New York: P Lang, 1996.

Cummings, Charles. *Eco-Spirituality.* New York: Paulist Press, 1991.

Deane-Drummond, Celia. *The Ethics of Nature.* Malden, MA: Blackwell Publications, 2004.

Deane-Drummond, Celia. *Ecology in Jurgen Moltmann's Theology.* Lewiston, NY: Edwin Mellen, 1997.

Deane-Drummond, Celia. *A Handbook in Theology and Ecology* London: SCM Press, 1996.

Derr, Thomas S. *Ecology and Human Need.* Philadelphia: Westminster Press, 1975.

Derr, Thomas S. *Environmental Ethics and Christian Humanism.* Nashville, TN: Abingdon Press, 1996.

Derr, Thomas S. *The Complexity and Ambiguity of Environmental Stewardship.* Response in DeWitt, Calvin B. 1998. "Caring for Creation: Responsible Stewardship of God's Handiwork". Grand Rapids, MI: Barker Book House, 1998.

Derr, Thomas S, with Nash, James A and Neuhaus, Richard J. *Environmental Ethics and Christian Humanism.* Nashville: Abingdon Press, 1996.

Derrick, C. *The Delicate Creation.* Old Greenwich, Conn.: Devin-Adair Co., 1972.

DeWitt, Calvin B. *Caring for Creation: Responsible Stewardship of God's Handiwork* Grand Rapids, MI: Barker Book House, 1998.

DeWitt, Calvin B. *Earthwise: a Biblical Response to Environmental Issues.* Grand Rapids, Mich: CRC Publications, 1994.

Dickson, John P. *Mission-commitment in Ancient Judaism and in the Pauline Communities: the shape, extent and background of early Christian Mission.* Tubingen: Mohr Siebeck, 2003.

Diesendorf, Mark. *Greenhouse Solutions with Sustainable Energy.* Sydney, Aust: UNSW Press, 2007.

Donovan, Vincent. *The Church in the Midst of Creation.* Maryknoll, NY: Orbis Books, 1992.

Dorr, Donal. *Mission in Today's World.* Maryknoll, New York: Orbis Books, 2000.

Dorr, Donal. *The Social Justice Agenda: Justice, Ecology, Power, and the Church.* Melbourne: Collins Dove, 1991.

Duchrow, Ulrich & Liedke, Gerhard. *Shalom: Biblical Perspectives on Creation, Justice, and Peace* Geneva: WCC Publications, 1989.

Dupont Alan, Pearman Graeme. *Heating up the Planet: Climate Change and Security.* Double Bay, NSW: Lowy Institute for International Policy, 2006.

Dutney, Andrew. *Creation and the Church: Proposals and Prospects for an Ecological Ecclesiology.* In Trinity Occasional Papers, Vol 6 (2), 1987.

Edwards, Denis ed. *Earth Revealing, Earth Healing: Ecology and Christian Theology.* Collegeville, Minn: Liturgical Press, 2001.

Edwards, Denis. *Ecology at the Heart of Faith: The Change of Heart that leads to a New Way of Living on Earth.* Maryknoll, New York: Orbis Books, 2006.

Edwards, Denis. *Called to be the Church in Australia: an approach to the renewal of local churches.* Homebush, NSW: St Paul Publications, 1987.

Edwards, Denis. *Jesus the Wisdom of God: an Ecological Theology.* (Aust. Edition) Homebush, NSW: St Paul's, 1995.

Edwards, Denis and Worthing, Mark eds. *Biodiversity and Ecology as Interdisciplinary Challenge.* Adelaide, SA: Australian Theological Forum.

Flannery, Tim. *The Weather Makers: The History and Future Impact of Climate Change.* Melbourne: Text Publishing, 2005.

Forrester, Duncan B. *Truthful Action: Explorations in Practical Theology.* Edinburgh: T & T Clark, 2000.

Fowler, James W. *Practical Theology and the Shaping of Christian Lives.* In Browning, Don S ed. *Practical Theology* San Francisco: Harper & Row, 1983.

Fowler, Robert B. *The Greening of Protestant Thought.* Chapel Hill & London: The University of North Carolina Press, 1995.

Fox M. *The Coming of the Cosmic Christ.* North Blackburn, Vic.: Collins Dove, 1988.

Fretheim, Terence E. *The Book of Genesis.* In "The New Interpreters Bible", Vol 1, Nashville: Abingdon Press, 1994.

Galvin R and Kearns R eds. *Repainting the Rainbow: Ecology and Christian Living.* Auckland: University of Auckland, 1989.

Gibbs, John: *Pauline Cosmic Christology and Ecological Crisis.* In Fitzmyer, J.A. ed. "Journal of Biblical Literature", Missoula, MT: University of Montana, Vol 90, p466-479, 1971.

Gnanakan, Ken. *God's World: Biblical Insights for a Theology of the Environment.* London: SPCK, 1999.

Gore, Al. *Earth in the Balance: Economy and the Human Spirit.* New York: Plume, 1993.

Gormley, Michael. *Our Quest for Ecological Integrity.* ASCIC, 2000.

Gottlieb, Roger S. ed. *This Sacred Earth: Religion, Nature, Environment.* New York: Routledge, 1996.

Graham, Larry K. *Care of Persons, Care of Worlds: a Psychosystems Approach to Pastoral Care and Counseling.* Nashville: Abingdon Press, 1992.

Granberg-Michaelson, Wesley. *Redeeming the Creation.* Geneva: WCC Publications, 1992.

Granberg-Michaelson, Wesley. *Worldly Spirituality: The Call to Redeem Life on Earth.* San Francisco: Harper and Row, 1984.

Gregorios, Paulos. *The Human Presence: an Orthodox View of Nature.* Geneva: WCC Publications, 1978.

Guatta, Winifred. *Environment.* Caufield East, Vic.: Dove Communications, 1973.

Gustafson, James M. *A Sense of the Divine: the Natural Environment from a Theocentric Perspective.* Edinburgh: T & T Clark, 1994.

Habel, Norman C and Balabanski, Vicki eds. *The Earth Story in the New Testament.* Sheffield: Sheffield Academic Press, 2002.

Habel, Norman *Rainbow of Mysteries: Meeting the Sacred in Nature.* Kelowna BC, Canada: CooperHouse (Wood Lake Pub), 2012.

Habel, Norman C. *Readings from the Perspective of Earth.* Sheffield: Sheffield Academic Press, 2000.

Habel, Norman C and Wurst, Shirley eds. *The Earth Story in Genesis.* Sheffield: Sheffield Academic Press, 2000.

Habel, Norman C. *The Third Mission of the Church*. In "Trinity Occasional Papers" (Trinity Theological College, Brisbane) XVII, I, pp31-43, 1998.

Halkes, Catharina J M. *New Creation: Christian Feminism and the Renewal of the Earth*. London: SPCK, 1991.

Hall, Douglas John. *Imaging God: Dominion as Stewardship*. Grand Rapids, MI: Eerdmans Publishing, 1986.

Hall, Douglas John. *Stewardship as Key to a Theology of Nature*. In Berry R.J. (ed) "Environmental Stewardship". London and New York: T & T Clark, 2006.

Hall, Douglas John and Ruether Rosemary Radford. *God and the Nations*. Minneapolis, MN.: Fortress Press, 1995.

Hallman DG ed. *Ecotheology: Voices from South and North*. Geneva, WCC Publications, and New York: Orbis Books, 1994.

Hallman DG. *Spiritual Values for Earth Community*. Geneva: WCC Publications, 2000.

Hamilton, Clive. *Earth Masters: Playing God with the Climate*. Crows Nest, NSW: Allen and Unwin, 2013.

Hammond, Catherine ed. *Creation Spirituality in the Dreamtime*. Newtown, NSW: Millennium Books, 1991.

Harrison, Peter. *Having Dominion: Genesis and the Mastery of Nature*. In Berry, R J ed. 2006. "Environmental Stewardship: Critical Perspectives – Past and Present". London and New York: T & T Clark International, 2006.

Hart, John. *What are They Saying about Environmental Theology?* Mahwah, New Jersey: Paulist Press, 2004.

Haught, John F. *The Promise of Nature: Ecology and Cosmic Purpose*. New York, NY: Paulist Press, 1993.

Hayes, Zachary. *The Gift of Being: a Theology of Creation*. Collegeville, Minn.: Liturgical Press, 2000.

Heldt, Jean-Paul. *Revisiting the 'Whole Gospel': Toward a Biblical Model of Holistic Mission in the 21st Century.* "Missiology: An International Review"; Vol XXXII, No 2, pp 149-172, April 2004.

Hessel, Dieter T ed. *After Nature's Revolt: Eco-justice and Theology.* Minneapolis: Fortress Press, 1992.

Hessel, Dieter T ed. *For Creation's Sake: Preaching, Ecology, and Justice. 1st edn.* Philadelphia: Geneva Press, 1985.

Hessel, Dieter T ed. *The Church's Public Role: Retrospect and Prospect.* Grand Rapids, Mich.: Wm B Eerdmans Publishing Co, 1993.

Hessel, Dieter T & Reuther, Rosemary Radford eds. *Christianity and Ecology: Seeking the Well-being of Earth and Humans.* Cambridge, Mass: Harvard University Press, 2000.

Houghton, John. (i). *Global Warming, Climate Change and Sustainability: Challenge to Scientists, Policy Makers, and Christians.* Cheltenham UK: John Ray Initiative. (Briefing Paper 14), 2007.

Houghton, John. (ii). *IPCC Fourth Assessment Report (FAR), Summary for Policymakers.* John Ray Initiative website, 2007.

Hume, Lynne. *The Rainbow Serpent, The Cross, and the Fax Machine: Australian Aboriginal Responses to the Bible.* In Brett, Mark G. ed. *Ethnicity and the Bible.* Leiden: E.J. Brill, 1996.

Jenkinson, William, and O'Sullivan, Helene eds. *Trends in Mission: towards the 3rd millennium.* Maryknoll, New York: Orbis Books, 1991.

John Knox International Reformed Centre. *Witnessing in the Midst of a Suffering Creation.* Geneva: John Knox Centre, 2007.

John Paul 11, Pope. *Peace with God the Creator, Peace with all of Creation.* Australian ed., Homebush, NSW: St Paul Publications, 1990.

John Paul 11, Pope. *The Gospel of Life.* New York: Random House, 1995.

Johnson, Eleanor and Clark, John eds. *Anglicans in Mission: a Transforming Journey.* London: SPCK, 2000.

Johnson, Elizabeth A. *Women, Earth, and Creator Spirit.* New York, NY: Paulist Press, 1993.

Joranson, Philip N. *Cry of the Environment: Rebuilding the Christian Creation Tradition.* Santa Fe: Bear, 1984.

Kalof, Linda and Satterfield, Terre. *The Earthscan Reader in Environmental Values.* London; Sterling VA: Earthscan, 2005.

King, Carolyn M. *Habitat of Grace: Biology, Christianity, and the Global Environmental Crisis.* Hindmarsh, SA: Australian Theological Forum, 2002.

Kinsler, Ross. *The Biblical Jubilee and the Struggle for Life: an invitation to personal, ecclesial, and social transformation.* Maryknoll, New York: Orbis Books, 1999.

Kinsley, David R. *Ecology and Religion: Ecological Spirituality in Cross-Cultural Perspective.* Englewood Cliffs, N.J.: Prentice Hall, 1995.

Kirk, J Andrew. *What is Mission? Theological Explorations.* London: Darton, Longman and Todd Ltd, 1999.

Knitter, Paul F. *One Earth, Many Religions: Multifaith Dialogue and Global Responsibility.* Maryknoll, New York: Orbis Books, 1996.

Knitter, Paul F. *Jesus and Other Names: Christian Mission and Global Responsibility.* Maryknoll, New York: Orbis Books, 1996.

Krueger, Frederick W ed. *Christian Ecology: Building an Environmental Ethic for the Twenty-first Century.* North American Conference on Christianity and Ecology, 1988.

LaChance, Albert J and Carroll, John E. *Embracing Earth: Catholic Approaches to Ecology.* Maryknoll NY: Orbis Books, 1994.

Langmead, Ross. *Rethinking Mission in Australia.* Melbourne: Australian Missiology Conference, 2005.

Larkin William J Jnr & Williams Joel F eds. 1998. *Mission in the New Testament: an Evangelical Approach.* Maryknoll, New York: Orbis Books, 1998.

Leal, Robert Barry. *Negativity towards Wilderness in the Biblical Record.* In "Ecotheology: Journal of Religion, Nature and the Environment" p 364-381. London: Equinox Publishing, 2005.

Leal, Robert Barry. *The Environment and Christian Faith: An Introduction to Eco-theology.* Strathfield NSW: St Paul's Publications, 2004.

Leal, Robert Barry. *Through Ecological Eyes: Reflections on Christianity's Environmental Credentials.* Strathfield NSW: St Paul's Publications, 2006.

Limouris, Gennadios. *Justice Peace and the Integrity of Creation: Insights from Orthodoxy.* Geneva: WCC Publications, 1990.

Louw, DJ. *Dreaming the Land in Hope: towards a practical theological ecclesiology of cura terrae.* Unpublished paper delivered in Brisbane, 2005.

Lowe, Ian. *Living in the Hothouse: how global warming affects Australia.* Melbourne: Scribe Publications, 2005.

Macquarrie, John. *Principles of Christian Theology* (Revised Edition). London: SCM Press, 1977.

McDaniel, Jay B. *With Roots and Wings: Christianity in an age of Ecology and Dialogue.* Maryknoll, NY: Orbis Books, 1995.

McDaniel, Jay B. *Earth, Sky, Gods, and Mortals: Developing an Ecological Spirituality.* Mystic, Conn.: Twenty-Third Publications, 1990.

McDonagh, Sean. *To Care for the Earth: A Call to a New Theological Passion for the Earth.* London: Geoffrey Chapman, 1986.

McDonagh, Sean. *Passion for the Earth: the Christian Vocation to Promote Justice, Peace, and the Integrity of Creation.* London: Geoffrey Chapman, 1994.

McDonagh, Sean. *The Greening of the Church.* Scoresby, Vic: Canterbury Press, 1990.

McFague, Sallie. *Life Abundant: Rethinking Theology and Economy for a Planet in Peril.* Minneapolis; London, Fortress Press, 2001.

McFague, Sallie. *Models of God: Theology for an Ecological, Nuclear Age.* Philadelphia: Fortress Press, 1987.

McFague, Sallie. *Super, Natural Christians: How we should love nature.* London: SCM Press, 1997.

McFague, Sallie. *The Body of God: an Ecological Theology.* Minneapolis; London: Fortress; SCM, 1993.

McGrath, Alister. *The Re-enchantment of nature: Science, Religion, and the Human Sense of Wonder.* London: Hodder & Stoughton, 2002.

McGregor, Ian. *An Ecologically Sustainable Business Sector Within An Ecologically Sustainable Society.* Auckland: Ecological Economics Think Tank, 2003.

Maguire, Daniel C and Rasmussen, Larry L. *Ethics for a Small Planet: New Horizons on Population, Consumption, and Ecology.* Albany, N.Y.: State University of New York Press, 1998.

Martin-Schramm, James B. *Christian Environmental Ethics: a Case Method Approach.* Maryknoll, NY: Orbis Books, 2003.

Mead, Loren B. *Transforming Congregations for the Future.* Washington DC: The Alban Institute, 1994.

Mead, Loren B. *The Once and Future Church.* Washington DC: The Alban Institute, 1991.

Mead, Loren B. *Five Challenges for the Once and Future Church.* Washington DC: The Alban Institute, 1996.

Migliore, Daniel L. *The Missionary God and the Missionary Church.* Princeton Seminary Bulletin, Vol XIX No 1, New Series, pp 14-25, 1998.

Miller, G Tyler. *Living in the Environment.* Belmont, CA: Wadsworth, 1982.

Mission and Public Affairs Council. *Sharing God's Planet: a Christian vision for a sustainable future.* London: Church House Publishing, 2005.

Moltmann, J. *God in Creation: An Ecological Doctrine of Creation.* London: SCM Press Ltd, 1985.

Moltmann, J. *Creating a Just Future: the Politics of Peace and the Ethics of Creation in a threatened World.* London; Philadelphia: SCM; Trinity Press International, 1989.

Moltmann, J. *The Church in the Power of the Spirit.* London: SCM Press, 1998.

Murphy, Charles M. *At Home on Earth: Foundations for a Catholic Ethic of the Environment.* New York: Crossroad, 1989.

Nash, James. *Loving Nature: Ecological Integrity and Christian Responsibility.* Nashville: Abingdon, 1991.

Nash, Roderick. *The Rights of Nature: A History of Environmental Ethics.* Leichhardt NSW: Primavera Press, 1991.

Niles, D Preman ed. *Between the Flood and the Rainbow: Interpreting the Conciliar Process of Mutual Commitment (Covenant) to Justice, Peace and the Integrity of Creation.* Geneva: WCCPublications, 1992.

Northcott, Michael S. *The Environment and Christian Ethics.* Cambridge: Cambridge University Press, 1996.

O'Day, Gail R. *The Gospel of John.* In *New Interpreters Bible, Vol 9,* Nashville: Abingdon Press, 1995.

Oelschlaeger, Max. *Caring for Creation: an Ecumenical Approach to the Environmental Crisis.* Newhaven, Conn.: Yale Univ Press, 1994.

Ogletree, Thomas W. *Dimensions of Practical Theology: Meaning, Action, Self.* In Browning, Don S ed. *Practical Theology* San Francisco: Harper & Row, 1983.

Osborn, Lawrence. *Guardians of Creation: Nature in Theology and the Christian Life.* Leicester: Apollos, 1993.

Palmer, Clare. *Environmental Ethics and Process Thinking.* Oxford: Clarendon Press, 1998.

Passmore, John. *Man's Responsibility for Nature: Ecological Problems and Western Traditions.* London: Duckworth, 1974.

Phillips, James M and Coote, Robert T eds. *Towards the 21st Century in Christian Mission.* Grand Rapids, Michigan: Wm B Eerdmans Publishing Co, 1993.

Pinches, Charles, & McDaniel, Jay B eds. *Good News for Animals? Christian approaches to animal well-being.* Maryknoll NY: Orbis Books, 1993.

Presbyterian Eco-Justice task Group. *Keeping and Greening the Creation.* Louisville, KY: Committee on Social Witness Policy, Presbyterian Church, USA, 1989.

Primavesi, Anne. *From Apocalypse to Genesis: Ecology, Feminism, and Christianity* Minneapolis; Tunbridge Wells, Kent: Fortress press; Burns and Oates, 1991.

Quinn, Frederick. *To Heal the Earth: a Theology of Ecology.* Nashville: Upper Room Books, 1994.

Rasmussen, Larry L. *Earth Community, Earth Ethics.* Geneva: WCC Publications, 1996.

Rhoads, David M. *The Role of the Church in the Care of the Earth.* Currents in Theology and Mission, 18 D, p406-414, 1991.

Roberts, B.R. *Sustainable Land Use: What can a Christian Land Ethic do?"* Unpublished paper, Australasian Rural Ministry Conference, Waipawa, New Zealand, 1992.

Roberts, W Dayton. *Patching God's Garment: Environment and Mission in the 21st Century.* Monrovia, CA: MARC, 1994.

Royal, Robert. *The Virgin and the Dynamo: use and abuse of religion in environmental debates.* Washington DC: Ethics and Public Policy Center, and Grand Rapids, Mich.: W.B. Eerdmans, 1999.

Rue, Charles. *Climate Change – Mapping an Australian Catholic Response.* Unpublished paper, 2008.

Ruether, Rosemary Radford. *Gaia and God: an ecofeminist theology of earth healing.* San Francisco: HarperSanFrancisco, 1992.

Ruether, Rosemary Radford. *Sexism and God-Talk: Toward a Feminist Theology.* Boston: Beacon Press, 1993.

Sanford, Agnes. *Creation Waits.* Plainfield, NJ: Logos International, 1977.

Santmire, H Paul. *In God's Ecology: a revisionist theology of nature.* In "Christian Century" Dec 13, 2000, pp 1300-1305, 2000.

Santmire, H Paul. *The Travail of Nature – the Ambiguous Ecological Promise of Christian Theology.* Minnealopolis, MN: Fortress Press, 1985.

Santmire, H Paul. *Nature Reborn: the Ecological and Cosmic Promise of Christian Theology*. Minneapolis: Fortress Press, 2000.

Scharper, Stephen B. *Redeeming the Time: a Political Theology of the Environment*. New York: Continuum, 1998.

Sheldon, Joseph K. *Rediscovery of Creation: a Bibliographical Study of the Church's Response to the Environmental Crisis*. Metuchen, NJ: American Theological Library Association, Scarecrow Press, 1992.

Shenk, Wilbert R. *Changing Frontiers of Mission*. Maryknoll, New York: Orbis Books, 1999.

Shrader-Frechette, KS. *Environmental Ethics*. Pacific Grove, CA: Boxwood Press, 1991.

Simkins, Ronald A. *Creator and Creation*. Peabody, Mass.: Hendrickson Publishing, 1994.

Sittler, Joseph. *Called to Unity*. In Ecumenical Review, Vol 14 No. 2, (Geneva, WCC Publications), p177-187, Jan 1962.

Smith, Pamela. *What are they Saying about Environmental Ethics?* New York: Paulist Press, 1997.

Smith, Paul R. *it Okay to Call God "Mother": Considering the Feminine Face of God*. Peabody, Mass.: Hendrickson Publishers, 1993.

Spencer, Nick, and White, Robert. *Christianity, Climate Change and Sustainable Living*. London: SPCK, 2007.

Stanislaus, L. *Ecology: An Awareness for Mission* SEDOS Bulletin, 31 D, p320-327, 1999.

Stern, Nicholas. *The Stern Review: The Economics of Climate Change (Executive Summary.)*, 2006.

Strong, DH, and Rosenfield. *Ethics or Expediency: an Environmental Question*. In Shrader-Frechette, KS. "Environmental Ethics". Pacific Grove, CA: Boxwood Press, 1991.

Thomas, Norman ed. *Readings in World Mission*. London: SPCK, 1995.

Tracy, David. *The Analogical Imagination: Christian Theology and the Culture of Pluralism*. London: SCM Press, 1981.

Tracy, D. *Blessed Rage for Order: The New Pluralism in Theology.* New York: Seabury Press (Crossroads), 1975.

Tracy, D. *The Foundations of Practical Theology.* In Browning, Don S ed. 1983. *Practical Theology* San Francisco: Harper & Row, 1983.

Treston, Kevin. *Creation Theology: Theology of Creation.* Samford, Qld: Creation Enterprises, 1990.

Treston, Kevin. *Walk Lightly upon the Earth: Christian Spirituality for Daily Living.* Wilston, Qld: Creation Enterprises, 2003.

Uniting Church in Australia. *Healing the Earth: An Australian Christian Reflection on the Renewal of Creation.* St James, NSW: UCA Assembly Social Responsibility and Justice Committee, 1990.

Van Dyke, Fred, Mahan, David C, Sheldon, Joseph K, Brand, Raymond H. *Redeeming Creation: the Biblical Basis for Environmental Stewardship.* Downers Grove, Illinois: InterVarsity Press, 1996.

Van Hoogstraten, Hans Dirk. *Deep Economy: Caring for Ecology, Humanity, and Religion.* Cambridge: James Clarke and Co, 2001.

Vogel, Steven. *Against Nature: the Concept of Nature in Critical Theory.* Albany, New York: State University of New York Press, 1996.

Walker, Christopher. *Seeking Relevant Churches for the 21ˢᵗ Century.* Melbourne: JBCE Books, 1997.

Westermann, Claus. *Creation.* London: SPCK, 1971.